SHARPEN YOUR TEAM'S SKILLS IN

PEOPLE SKILLS

Other titles in this series

Sharpen your skills in motivating people to perform
Trevor Bentley 007 709072 1

Sharpen your team's skills in effective selling
Trevor Bentley   007 709279 1

Sharpen your team's skills in developing strategy
Susan Clayton   007 709281 3

Sharpen your team's skills in supervision
Susan Clayton   007 709092 8

Sharpen your team's skills in creativity
Trevor Bentley   007 709282 1

Sharpen your team's skills in coaching
Tony Voss   007 709278 3

Sharpen your team's skills in project management
Jean Harris   007 709140 X

Sharpen your team's skills in time management
Jane Allan   007 709275 9

SHARPEN YOUR TEAM'S SKILLS IN

*P*EOPLE SKILLS

Di Kamp

The McGraw-Hill Companies

London · New York · St Louis · San Francisco · Auckland · Bogotá · Caracas
Lisbon · Madrid · Mexico · Milan · Montreal · New Delhi · Panama · Paris
San Juan · São Paulo · Singapore · Sydney · Tokyo · Toronto

Published by
McGraw-Hill Publishing Company
Shoppenhangers Road, Maidenhead, Berkshire, SL6 2QL, England
Telephone 01628 502500
Facsimile 01628 770224

British Library Cataloguing in Publication Data
Kamp, Di,
   Sharpen your team's skills in people skills
   1. Personnel management 2. Interpersonal relations
   I. Title II. People skills
   658.3'145

ISBN 007 709276 7

Library of Congress Cataloging-in-Publication Data
Kamp, Di,
   Sharpen your team's skills in people skills / Di Kamp.
     p. cm.
   Includes index.
   ISBN 0-07-709276-7 (pbk. : alk. paper)
   1. Personnel management–Study and teaching. 2. Interpersonal
relations–Study and teaching. 3. Personnel management–Problems,
exercises, etc. 4. Interpersonal relations–Problems, exercises,
etc. I. Title.
HF5549.15.K36   1996
658.3–dc20   96–34473
                                   CIP

McGraw-Hill

A Division of The *McGraw·Hill* Companies

12345 CUP 9987

Typeset by BookEns Ltd, Royston, Herts
Printed and bound in Great Britain at the University Press, Cambridge

Printed on permanent paper in compliance with ISO Standard 9706

CONTENTS

SCENARIOS

EXERCISES

Series Preface

This series of books focuses on helping you to improve the performance of your team by providing a range of training and support materials. These materials can be used in a variety of ways to improve the knowledge and skills of your team.

The creation of high performance is achieved by paying attention to three key elements:

- the skills or competencies of your people;
- the way these skills are applied;
- the support your people receive from you in applying their skills.

SKILL DEVELOPMENT

The books in this series will provide materials for the development of a range of skills on a subject by subject basis. Each book will provide information and exercises in manageable chunks or lessons, which will be presented in a format that will allow you to choose the most appropriate way to deliver it to your staff. The contents will consist of all you need to guide your staff to a full understanding of the subject.

There are at least four ways you could choose to guide the learning of your team:

- training sessions
- learning groups
- open learning
- experiential learning.

TRAINING SESSIONS

These can be run by bringing your people together and guiding them step by step through the materials, including the exercises. During these sessions you can invite your people to interact with you and the materials by asking questions and relating the materials to their current work. The materials will provide you with the detailed information you need to present the subject to your team.

LEARNING GROUPS

This approach involves dividing your team into small groups of two, three or four people and having a brief session with each group, introducing them to the materials. Each group then works through the materials and meets with you from time to time to assess progress and receive your guidance.

OPEN LEARNING

This approach invites your people to use the materials at their own speed and in their own way. This is a form of individual learning that can be managed by regular meetings between you and your team as individuals or in a group. The process is started by introducing the materials to your team and agreeing some 'learning outcomes' to be achieved.

EXPERIENTIAL LEARNING

This calls for you to invite your team to examine the materials using the exercises as a focus, and then to get them to relate what they are learning directly to real-life situations in the workplace. This experience of learning is then shared and discussed by the team as a whole.

The books in the series have been designed to enable these four approaches to be used as well as other ways that you might think are more appropriate to your team's specific needs.

APPLYING SKILLS

Time spent developing skills can be wasted if people do not have the opportunity to practise them. It is important that you consider this aspect of performance before embarking on a particular programme. It is useful if you are able to clearly identify opportunities for practising skills and to discuss these with your team. Providing opportunities for practising and further developing competency is part and parcel of the whole approach of this series.

PROVIDING SUPPORT

Once people have acquired a new skill and have been provided with opportunities to apply it, they still need your support and coaching while they are experimenting with using it. The opening book in this series, *Sharpen Your Skills in Motivating People to Perform*, provides clear guidance on how to help people to develop their skills and then how to provide experience, practice and support as they use these skills.

Before starting work with your team on the materials in this book I suggest you do the following:

1. Review the materials yourself.
2. Plan the approach you are going to follow.
3. Discuss with your team what you are planning.
4. Agree some learning outcomes.
5. Indicate how you are going to support your team during the learning process.

The authors in the series have endeavoured to provide a range of materials that is comprehensive and will support you and your team. I hope that during this process you learn from and enjoy the experience.

Dr Trevor J. Bentley
Series Editor

ABOUT THE EDITORIAL PANEL

Dr Trevor Bentley, series editor for this series, is a freelance organizational consultant, a facilitator and a writer. Prior to becoming a consultant and while working as a senior executive, Trevor carried out a major research project into decision making and organization structures for which he was awarded his PhD. Over the last 20 years he has had a wide range of experience working with organizations in over 20 countries. Trevor has trained for four years with Gestalt South West and has attended Gestalt workshops in the UK and Europe. He now applies a Gestalt approach in his work.

Trevor has written 20 books and over 250 articles on business-related issues. His background includes careers as a management accountant, financial director, computer systems designer, a management services manager, a human-computer interface consultant, a trainer and a business manager. His current area of interest is in the application of a Gestalt approach to solving problems of organizational harmony. This includes culture change, performance management, team facilitation, executive coaching, mentoring and integrated supervision.

Susan Clayton is a leading contributor to the use and development of Gestalt philosophy and practice in organizations. Focusing on human processes, she enables managers and their staff to achieve business goals that depend on managing people. Her skill in raising awareness of how people relate to each other can forge supportive alliances and powerful co-operative relationships. Her approach includes helping people to manage blocks and difficulties in their contact with others, clearing the way for work and business relationships to move forward and grow.

Susan works with managers at all levels. Her interventions have aided groups in turmoil, managers needing to reach common agreement and individuals needing mentoring and coaching support. She helps organizations understand how to manage in a way that creates trust, respect and clarity in human relationships.

Mike Taylor is a consultant involved in the design, implementation and facilitation of personal and team development programmes within organizations. After graduating in 1987, he has worked with two outdoor management training providers, both as a manager and tutor. His work has a strong focus on the use of experiential learning in developing managers, mainly within larger organizations.

He also works with groups and single individuals in running meetings and events that help teams and individuals explore working practices and approaches. More recently he has developed an interest in Gestalt as a way of understanding group processes. He is a member of the Association for Management Education and Development.

Dr Tony Voss is a counsellor, consultant and trainer. He originally trained as a chemist before working in environmental research developing sea-going computer systems and information technology, and later in the computer industry as a project manager, consultant and quality manager. Tony has a particular interest in enabling people to contribute fully and creatively to their endeavours, and sees this as benefiting individuals, their organizations and society at large. He is an Accredited Counsellor with the British Association for Counselling, and has also trained in Gestalt over four years.

Tony works with those wanting to develop their organizations and people, and those dealing with particular challenges in their working life. His clients also include those exploring the role of work in their life, as well as those with more personal issues.

*A*BOUT THE AUTHOR

Di Kamp is a training consultant with blue-chip companies, specializing in change, enhancing performance and management skills. She has many years' experience of working with teams on people skills and developing the key techniques that make a difference. Her previous publications include *50 Management Development Activities* (Gower), *25 Role Plays for Managers* (Gower), *Triggers for Time Management* (Gower), *The Excellent Trainer* (Gower), *Successful Staff Appraisals in a Week* (Hodder & Stoughton), and *Workplace Counselling* (McGraw-Hill).

Acknowledgements

This book is the result of many years of exploring this topic, both overtly and covertly, with many different people.

I would like to thank my teachers who have helped me to develop my own people skills, in particular, John Grinder and Ram Dass.

I would also like to acknowledge all those who have learned with me on courses and development programmes, who have both taught me and helped me to explore ways of putting this message across more effectively.

Finally, I would like to acknowledge the assistance of all the difficult people I have ever met, who have forced me to reconsider my own skills and continue to develop them.

Without the help of John Hume, the book would never have been completed. His dedication in word-processing for me, and checking out that I was making sense, at least to some degree, has helped enormously.

And, as ever, the staff at McGraw-Hill have proved to be supportive and helpful in bringing this book to fruition.

Di Kamp

CHAPTER 1

INTRODUCTION: WHY PEOPLE SKILLS?

WHAT ARE PEOPLE SKILLS?

We have devoted a whole book to developing the people skills of your staff. Yet it is not a subject which you find listed in many training plans. In fact, people skills sounds like something far removed from the business of getting things done, doesn't it! We tend to think of it as one of those 'soft' subjects that are finc for those who have time to spare, but that are not really relevant when you are busy trying to make things happen.

If you stop and think about it, you will realize that people skills are crucial in all business transactions. The subject is the approach that people use in their dealing with others. How we deal with other people affects how effective we are in performing most of our tasks at work, because few of us work in isolation from other people. Being able to manage your relationships at work, so that they have the effect you want, is a prerequisite of optimum performance.

HOW THE DEVELOPMENT OF PEOPLE SKILLS HELPS THE BUSINESS

The feeling that people skills are a luxury rather than a necessity has been increased by the fact that many training programmes in this area have emphasized the personal development involved. Your staff may come back from one feeling good about themselves, but there is no noticeable change in their work, and they soon lose the euphoria and revert to 'normal'. So why bother to look at this area, in the context of improving performance?

'PEOPLE ARE OUR GREATEST ASSETS'

More and more organizations are beginning to recognize that the people who work for them are their greatest asset. This recognition is given in mission statements and company policies. In a constantly changing world, people who are flexible and motivated, who are able to learn and develop, are invaluable. The trouble is, a lot of people don't seem to have these qualities at work. As one senior manager put it to me: 'Our people are our greatest asset, they say. What they don't say is that they are also our greatest problem!'

And one of the areas in which people in organizations are a problem is in the way they relate to each other – their people skills. Being good at the job is not enough, we also need people to get on with and co-operate with each other. This has always been the case. None of us work well in situations where there is back-biting and conflict, because they affect our mood, and our attitude. However, it is now becoming overtly recognized that when co-operation is 'the way we work here' the work performance is considerably enhanced.

Whatever your area of work, for the majority, work means working *with* and *for* other people. As we spend so much of our time at work, it makes sense to enhance the relationships, rather than to suffer the effects of poor ones.

SO WHAT ARE THE BENEFITS?

Enhancing interpersonal skills with your staff can bring with it noticeable gains on a variety of levels. There are benefits for you personally and professionally, there are benefits for your staff personally and professionally, there are benefits for the whole team, and there are benefits for the organization.

THE BENEFITS FOR YOU

As manager, you have to ensure that your 'unit' runs smoothly. Most managers I know would say that it isn't the task in hand that causes the headaches most of the time – it's dealing with all the day-to-day problems with people. If your staff have enhanced interpersonal skills, some of those problems disappear, and you have more time to devote to development, rather than 'mending'. You will also benefit from the improved 'atmosphere' that results from improved relationships.

The manager of a team I worked with expressed it like this: 'People smiling and saying "Hello" in the morning sounds unimportant, but I've found that it sets me up totally differently, and I set to with much more enthusiasm.'

You will also find that your staff relate to you differently. Enhanced interpersonal skills mean that they communicate with you more clearly and directly, so that it is easier to 'get the message', and also to 'give the message'.

Further, the very fact that you, the manager, have demonstrated that this topic matters to you, by working with them on enhancing their skills, will bring results. You cannot deal with this topic without showing a commitment to the principles of co-operation and respect. And that is something that your staff will respect you for. They will also tend to want to stay. We all know a good thing when we have it, and prefer working in a place where we feel valued.

Scenario – People skills matter

I remember a manager being very surprised when members of his team fed back to him their delight that he had encouraged them to look at ways of improving their relationships. He had thought that they would see it as a criticism. They saw it as proof that he didn't only care about the tasks being done, he also cared about them.

THE BENEFITS FOR YOUR STAFF

The last statement is one of the benefits for your staff – they feel cared about as people, by you. There are also personal gains, which it is important to emphasize with them.

- *Their differences are valued* As they increase their appreciation of each other, they will feel less pressure to 'conform' and more confidence in making their individual contributions.
- *Their confidence is increased* As they find that the strategies for improving relationships work, they will become more confident of their ability to deal with other people effectively.
- *Their working life is easier* When interpersonal skills are enhanced, there is less conflict, and they will find that they can get on with the job with less hassle.
- *The 'atmosphere' improves* As I pointed out earlier, everyone benefits when the general atmosphere at work is pleasant.
- *They will find it easier to express their point of view* By enhancing their interpersonal skills, they learn how to give their opinions constructively, and know that they will be listened to.
- *They will find it easier to deal with 'awkward customers'* The strategies we will look at will help them to be able to deal with difficult interpersonal situations more effectively.
- *They will enjoy work more* This is the obvious by-product of the previous benefits, but worth stating overtly.

■ *They will feel more enthusiastic about their work* When we are enjoying our work situation, and getting on with others around us, we tend to work far more effectively. This makes us feel good, as well as pleasing the bosses!

I'm still astonished that it comes as such a shock to people that improving work relationships can make such a significant difference to how the work is done and how they feel about it. We have all experienced the difference, in one setting or another, yet we don't consciously register what it is.

Scenario – The effect of relationships at work

I remember, many years ago, moving from one job to another, and wondering what had hit me. I had come from a place where we knew each other by our first names, where staff meetings were fun, and we all contributed. We all celebrated if someone had a success, and the way we got things done was by working together. The quiet one, the challenging one, the funny one, and the efficient one, were all valued. We even had the reputation of being able to 'smooth the rough diamonds' for the organization.

I moved to a place where everyone was known as Mr, Mrs, or Miss. Meetings were agonizing as faults were picked on, and people tried to keep out of the limelight. The constant threat of failure meant that people didn't talk about what they did, or co-operate. And we were all expected to behave in the same way. I didn't last long there.

We don't usually experience such marked contrasts (except when the family has had a major row!) but we do all of us experience some degree of this difference.

I now know that it is actually quite simple to make the changes necessary to turn the second situation round, if the manager decides that he or she wants to. And his or her staff are remarkably responsive to the lead, once they get past the initial suspicion!

BENEFITS FOR THE TEAM

Besides all the individual benefits from enhancing interpersonal skills, there are obviously benefits for the team as a whole.

When people work together in an atmosphere of mutual respect, they seem to produce a different 'synergy'. In other words, the total effect is more than the sum of the individual parts. We all get 'infected' by what's going on around us. If others are being co-operative, we tend to be. If others are daring to ask for help, we feel safer in doing so. If others pay attention to us and take us seriously, we tend to treat them the same.

So one benefit to the team as a whole is that they tend to help each other to maintain the good practice, rather than slide back into old habits. Further, this produces an environment in which the creativity of sharing and discussing ideas can flourish, so the team becomes more effective in its work.

Another way in which the team becomes more effective is in the use of the differences between them.

Scenario – Team benefits

An example of this is a senior management team I worked with. When they explored their differences and began to pay attention to the ways they each approached things, they realized that they could use those differences. Two of them tended to be very quiet in meetings, when the norm was to have a strong opinion. Those two became very valuable to the team: one was excellent at summarizing what had gone on, and the other was very perceptive in spotting when they had 'lost the thread' and were not going anywhere useful. When specifically asked to contribute their observations to the team, instead of being pressured to 'have opinions', they enhanced the productiveness of meetings significantly.

BENEFITS FOR THE ORGANIZATION

It's surely obvious, yet important to state overtly, that the organization will benefit. The cumulative effect of enhanced interpersonal skills for individuals is enhanced working practice. Not only do teams become more effective in their everyday tasks, they will also be far more likely automatically to begin to engage in continuous development – always a desired process for any organization.

As we are valued as individuals, and value others, as we become more confident of our views being received with respect and consideration, we begin to use our ability to innovate and improve.

This is demonstrated by the success of suggestion schemes. These have been introduced in many companies, but have not always been successful. The key difference is that those which work work because people feel that every suggestion is considered. And this 'feeling' can be traced back to the fact that there is clear feedback and recognition given to them.

Can we really claim that there can be so many benefits from enhancing people skills? I have no doubt that our people skills are fundamental in enhancing our performance. We all flourish in positive relationships with others.

Notice what a difference the 'right' teacher made to our enjoyment and learning in a particular subject at school. Notice how comfortable we feel with people who don't judge us or deride us – it's then that we will take risks, and try something different.

Compare different working situations you have experienced, and notice how powerfully relationships affect us.

Scenario – What makes the difference

I was asked to see if I could find out why absenteeism in a manufacturing plant varied so much from team to team. One of the team leaders I talked to expressed this very clearly. His team worked in what was regarded as one of the hardest areas, yet there was virtually no absenteeism. When I asked him why he thought this was so, he replied: 'I don't know. All I do is make sure that I get on with everyone in the team. And I help them to get on with each other, in whatever way I can. We like working together.'

As we continued talking, he told me how they had come up with their own ways of dealing with team briefings, individual training, arranging the work-load, etc. As far as he was concerned, his most important function was to create the 'we all get on' atmosphere. The rest just happened. For him, it was 'obvious' that people skills make a difference. And despite the fact that his team did clearly work well together, he still wanted more. He asked me how else he could improve their ways of getting on.

YOUR ROLE IN USING THIS BOOK

Some of you will not have thought before of consciously working with your staff to enhance their people skills. Others will be at a similar stage to the team leader in the last scenario, wondering if there is anything else you could do.

I would suggest that developing your staff in the area of people skills provides a useful foundation for any other development that you choose to do with them, or that they choose to undertake themselves.

The sessions covered in each chapter will give you a reference point when you take staff through some of the other subjects covered in this series.

WE ARE PRETTY GOOD ALREADY

You may feel that your team already work well together and that it is not necessary for you to explore this topic further.

I would propose that everyone can improve in this area, no matter where they start from, and that continuous improvement is the theme rather than just making a difference to a bad situation. This book is designed to give your team the opportunity to develop no matter what their starting point. And any improvement in this skills area provides tremendous pay-offs.

Scenario – The excellent team

Lin's team were already working well together. They were not sure that they wanted to explore ways of making further improvements. Lin pointed out to them that the situation at work was constantly changing, and that one of the changes was likely to be that they needed to work more closely with the design department. There was a general groan – the majority of them thought that people in the design department were a pain. She had made her point.

They embarked on the programme of development with some reluctance – how could it change their view of this other department? After a few sessions, Lin asked for feedback about the programme.

Phil spoke up for the rest when he said: 'I thought that this would be a waste of time, but already it has made me think about the way I treat others in **this** team, and certainly made me realize that there could be advantages in approaching the design department people with a different frame of mind to the one I held previously.'

EITHER YOU HAVE IT OR YOU HAVEN'T

A common myth about people skills is that you either can relate well to others or you can't. There is no doubt that some people find it easier than others, and have a natural bent towards creating effective relationships with others. This doesn't mean that skills in this area cannot be improved. In fact, we have probably all improved in our people skills since we were teenagers. We discover better ways of working with others by observing people who do it well, and we can also learn by taking the time to consider what works best for us, and using it more often.

This guide is designed to encourage people to learn from their own and other people's best practice.

WHAT THE BOOK CONSISTS OF

The book is divided into two parts:

- Fundamentals of people skills
- Applying people skills.

FUNDAMENTALS OF PEOPLE SKILLS

In this first part, we explore the basic skills that people can apply in any situation that requires people skills. There is an emphasis on how you set yourself up to relate well to others, and how you find out what will work to make the relationship useful for them as well.

APPLYING PEOPLE SKILLS

In the second part, we look at specific work situations where people often fall down in their use of people skills. We refer back to the most useful sections in Part 1 for the particular situations, and also add in some other strategies that people can use to help them to handle these more difficult encounters.

Although it would be possible to use the different chapters in a different order in Part 2, to suit the needs of your team, I would recommend that you go through Part 1 first, in the order given. It is planned to give a cumulative effect of improvement, and is referred to in the chapters in Part 2, so you need some familiarity with the material.

Part 2 can be taken in any order, according to the requirements of your team.

THE FORMAT OF THE CHAPTERS

The chapters are designed to be used in a variety of ways. Each one consists of text, examples (scenarios), and exercises. You can read through the chapter yourself, and add in your own comments, or your own examples, when you present it to your team, using the exercises to prompt them into consideration of how to apply the material. Alternatively, you can give them all copies and go through the material together – it is designed to be immediately usable. A further alternative would be to use the book as a self-study text, perhaps bringing the team together to do some of the exercises that involve them working together.

The examples are scenarios that illustrate the point being made. They are all taken from real experiences, although the names of those involved have been changed. You may choose to think up your own examples from your own immediate work situation.

There are also suggested action points at the end of each chapter for the whole team to try out. These are intended to prompt the team to put the points raised in the chapter into practice in their work. They could provide a useful beginning to each session that you hold – ask people to feed back what they have done differently since the last session.

Where I feel that you as manager need to be aware of certain points regarding the chapter, I have written in a few notes for your guidance. They may seem obvious to you, but I know how easy it is to get caught up in what you are doing, and not have time to go through the material beforehand. The notes should save you from hitting unforeseen problems once you are already involved.

This book is intended to make working life easier and

more enjoyable for you and your team. I hope that you have fun following this programme and find it of benefit to you.

PART 1

*F*UNDAMENTALS
OF PEOPLE SKILLS

CHAPTER 2

SELF-MANAGEMENT

KEY LEARNING POINTS

■ the importance of knowing how to control your own state
■ changing your mood
■ bringing out the best in yourself
■ appreciating your individuality

NOTES TO MANAGER/COACH

This first section is devoted to the need for people to be in the right state if they are to relate to others successfully. It will work best if you encourage people to examine their own good points thoroughly.

With Exercise 1, ask them to make brief notes on their examples individually. You may want to share a few examples in the group.

In Exercise 5, ask them to sit comfortably, and close their eyes. Then slowly read out the instructions to them. This exercise doesn't require any discussion.

In Exercise 8, do it individually, then ask everyone to share one thing they've thought of. Make it clear that this is to be received positively by the whole group, whatever they say, to encourage individuals to appreciate their own particular character traits.

WHY SELF-MANAGEMENT?

When we think of people skills, we usually think of how we handle other people, rather than how we handle ourselves. Yet all of us know that we are better or worse at relating to others, depending on our 'mood'. It is this mood or attitude that we are going to examine first.

If we can learn to control and change our own mood, we can improve our ability to relate to others. This means that we need to recognize how **we** affect what happens when we interact with others, and take responsibility for that effect.

Exercise 1 – The effect of your mood

Stop and think for a moment of three of your own examples, where your mood affected the way you dealt with other people.

Example

I was feeling really fed up, when my colleague asked me to help her with something. I agreed reluctantly, and began to find fault with what she had done. She became really defensive, and we didn't solve the problem.

CHANGING YOUR MOOD

We have been led to believe that we are how we are and there's nothing we can do about it. If our mood does change, we will claim that it is because something external has affected us. This lack of internal control over our state is an excuse rather than a reality. It is true that a change in external circumstances may change our mood, but it doesn't always happen.

Scenario – The apology

A colleague has promised to follow up with one of your customers while you are away. When you return, you discover that he hasn't done so, and you have an irate message from the customer.

You deal with the customer, and then go in search of your colleague. You are furious that he put you in the position of having to make excuses. Your colleague is very apologetic. He says that he tried to follow up, but got an engaged signal. Then he became totally absorbed in something else and forgot all about your customer. He is obviously upset at having let you down.

You calm down, and accept that it was just human error.

Or, you are still furious, and continue to rage at him about his behaviour, suggesting that this is typical of him, and wanting to make him feel even worse about it.

The reality is that we choose whether to change our mood or not, and while the external circumstances may influence our choice, they are not ever the reason for the mood. The reason for the mood is the way we are choosing to react to the situation. This may sound rather tough. It means that we have to take full responsibility for the mood we are in, and we can't blame external circumstances or other people. On the other hand, with the responsibility comes control. If we choose our mood, and we can learn how to do so consciously, then we can control the way we are, and use that to our advantage in any situation.

Exercise 2 – The benefits of a better mood

Take your three examples of affecting the interaction through your mood from Exercise 1. If you had chosen to be in a constructive mood for these interactions, what would have been the benefit to you?

Example

If I had approached my colleague's request in a constructive way, we would have solved the problem. She would have felt that I was interested and willing to help. I wouldn't have found fault, but would have given constructive suggestions. She would have valued even more my abilities, and we would have had an improved relationship. I would have felt good at the end because I had been able to help.

HOW TO CHOOSE YOUR MOOD

As it becomes attractive to think that you can choose your mood, it also raises the question of how we can do it. Most of the time we are not aware of how we choose our mood, and we have to learn how to make conscious choices.

We will look at this at two levels:

1. Feeling positive
2. Choosing the right situation.

FEELING POSITIVE

The basis for a constructive mood is feeling positive. We all know what a difference it makes to our day when we wake up feeling good. We deal with everything that happens in a constructive way.

We also tend to treat ourselves better. When we're in a good mood, we choose to wear clothes we like, we notice things that please us, we eat foods we enjoy. So when we already feel good, we do things that maintain the good feeling.

Conversely, when we're feeling bad, we tend to perpetuate that feeling: we put on clothes we don't like, because it doesn't matter, we deprive ourselves of enjoyable food, and we don't notice anything in the world around us, unless it contributes to our bad feelings!

Whatever state we are in, when we wake in the morning, we tend to perpetuate that same state, unless some external circumstance 'bounces' us out of it. This may be our habit, but it is quite easy to change it.

HOW TO MAKE YOURSELF FEEL POSITIVE

We can use quite simple techniques to make ourselves feel positive, and it doesn't require a great deal of effort. In fact, we have probably all done this when we were small children. We simply allow ourselves to have things that make us feel good!

Now, as adults, we associate such 'treats' with expense,

time, rarity value, etc. We have learnt to keep our treats for special occasions or as rewards for superior effort. Children, however, have a much simpler view. A treat is something that you receive through your senses that makes you feel good. So a child delights in a bright picture, the sound of a bird, the feel of sand between their toes, the smell of a flower, the taste of a freshly picked strawberry. And adults who are feeling good already have the same delight in these sensual treats.

Interestingly, making a conscious effort to identify and use these simple treats on an everyday basis works as well for adults as for children. In fact, we never totally left behind this way of feeling good. Most of us have made sure that the treats that we enjoy through our senses are available to us in our everyday lives, even if we don't actually use them. We have pictures and ornaments in our homes because we like the look of them; music in our CD collection that we love the sound of; perfumes and aftershaves and flowers in our gardens that we like the smell of; objects in our home and materials in our clothing that we like the feel of; and favourite foods and drinks to please our sense of taste.

Exercise 3 – Everyday treats

Take some time to think of everyday things that give you pleasure through your senses:

hearing
seeing
feeling/touching
tasting
smelling

Talk with others in your group about the treats you already have in your everyday life to make you feel good. Then identify with them four or five more that you could easily use to make you feel good when you weren't already in a good mood.

It is important to make sure that you identify some treats that are quick and easy to access for yourself. It's no good saying: 'I'd feel much better if I could soak in a perfumed bath for half an hour, with candles and soft music in the background.' It's a lovely treat, but not likely to be one you can access between meetings in your work day!

This may seem rather light-hearted to you – it's fun to identify treats, but now let's get down to the serious stuff. However, in my experience, those people who give themselves plenty of simple treats in a day are the people who keep themselves in a good state, and who deal with other people pleasantly and effectively.

If you want to feel good most of the time, then make sure that you have a regular supply of treats in your day:

- eat something you enjoy;
- have a picture at your desk that makes you smile when you look at it;
- go for a short walk round – that usually engages most of the senses;
- use your favourite aftershave/scent;
- keep a favourite cassette in the car.

By taking a moment to appreciate something that makes you smile, you add to your ability to choose to feel good. And remember to reverse our normal tendency: if you already feel good, have several extra treats to maintain that state; if you don't feel too good, have more treats, to change the mood; and if you feel downright bad, then overdose on treats, and you'll find it more and more difficult to resist feeling good.

CHOOSING THE RIGHT MOOD FOR THE SITUATION

Once we have established the habit of choosing to have a positive mood, we can add some refinements that allow us to choose an appropriate mood. After all, the type of feeling good that I have for a party may not be appropriate for an important meeting or for getting an urgent task done.

It is important that we learn how to set ourselves up to be in the 'right' mood for an activity or experience. Again, you will no doubt realize that sometimes we do this automatically. We don't think about it, it just happens. So what we need to do is to find out how we do it automatically, so that we can choose to do the same thing consciously, when it doesn't happen without us thinking about it.

HOW WE SET OURSELVES UP

What actually happens when we automatically set ourselves up in the right mood? It may be something we see in our mind's eye, or say to ourselves, that triggers us into adopting an appropriate physical and mental state, or it may be something we see or hear externally.

These triggers are our own personal way of reminding ourselves of what state to be in to suit the situation, and have been created as a result of earlier experiences of similar situations. They are very useful, as they give us an automatic pattern of behaviour in certain types of situations, so we don't always have to think about how we want to react and behave — if we had to plan it consciously each time, we would not do half as much in our days!

A simple example of the use of a trigger is the way we greet each other. When you see someone coming towards you that you know, you don't stop and think: 'What shall I do now?' You automatically switch into greeting mode, both verbally and physically.

No doubt you have already realized that sometimes these automatic triggers are not so useful. There are some situations where our trigger makes us feel defensive, or want to avoid whatever it is if at all possible.

The reason for this is that the trigger was created in a past experience of a similar situation. If the situation was one where you were defensive, or did want to avoid, then you will automatically recreate that state of mind.

For example, when I was young, I was called by my full name, Dianne, if I was in trouble. As a result, I still go into automatic defensive mode if someone calls me Dianne, and I have to readjust consciously, because it is not appropriate.

If, on the other hand, the experience was a positive or constructive one when you created the trigger, then you will automatically approach similar situations in a positive or constructive way.

Exercise 4 – Identifying triggers

I wonder if you can identify any triggers which you have. Think of some – no more than two that are negative, and at least four that are positive.

Example

If I hum Beethoven's 'Für Elise' to myself, I automatically calm down. If I picture myself on the stage at Wembley, I feel very confident.

Although normally these triggers are unconscious, it is worth starting to notice what triggers you into useful states, because then you can consciously choose to use them to create that state when you want to. In the examples I gave in Exercise 4, I have noticed things that create a useful state, and then can choose to use them. If I had to wait until I happened to hear the Beethoven piece, I wouldn't calm down very often! So instead I hum it to myself.

If you realize, for example, that being at the seaside makes you feel relaxed, then you can imagine yourself at the seaside to automatically trigger that relaxed state.

HOW TO CREATE NEW TRIGGERS

If you haven't found enough useful triggers to create just the right state for different situations, you can consciously make some to suit. This means that you can decide how you want to set yourself up for particular types of interactions, and then design a trigger to help you.

Exercise 5 – Creating new triggers

When you think about situations where a trigger would be useful, you will find that you have a mixture: some situations where you are fine, and some situations where you would like to be different. Examples are:

'I can get on with a new colleague, but I'm uncomfortable with a new boss.'
'I can relate to other women, but I feel awkward with men.'

'I can stand up and present to a group of strangers, but I'm really embarrassed if it is a group of colleagues.'

What are your examples? Write them out as in the examples above.

Now we're going to work through creating a trigger.

1. Choose one of your examples, and take the positive part, e.g. 'I can get on with a new colleague'. Think of a specific time when you experienced that.
2. Spend a few moments recalling the specific situation: who was there, where it took place, what it felt like. Then picture yourself in that situation: What was your body posture like? What expression did your face have? How mobile or still were you? Describe what you looked like in detail to yourself. This is what you look like when you have automatically triggered yourself into a useful state.
3. Now recall what was going on in your head. What were you thinking about the other person/people? What were you thinking about yourself? How would you describe your state of mind at that time? You now have a description of your useful mental state.
4. As you fully remember what you are like when you have set yourself up well, allow yourself to choose something to remind you of this state: it may be something you can see or picture to yourself; it may be something you say, or even sing to yourself!
5. Once you have chosen, say or picture this trigger to yourself and, as you do, recreate again exactly what you are like, physically and mentally, in the situation that went well.
6. Now take the second half of your statement: 'but I'm uncomfortable with a new boss'. Remember an experience of being in this situation. Notice briefly what you're like, physically and mentally, when you're feeling uncomfortable.
7. Now imagine the trigger you've created, and the physical and mental state that go with it. Change the previous version of you with the new boss, or whatever your situation is, to this new version, triggered to be able to get

on well. Notice how much better you feel in that experience with this different you.

8. Now imagine the next time you'll meet this type of situation, and see and hear yourself going into it in this new, useful way, by using your trigger.

9. From now on, whenever you want to, you can think of that trigger, and your body and mind will automatically go into that mode.

Now you have the basic mechanisms to set yourself up to approach others with the appropriate attitude. This gives you control over yourself and your moods, so that you begin any encounter feeling ready for it.

WHAT WE TELL OURSELVES

If you're not careful, however, you can find yourself losing that state very quickly, just because you tell yourself that it won't work! What we tell ourselves is very powerful in affecting our state. We think they are 'just thoughts', but those thoughts can instantly change our mood.

Scenario – Not a useful thought

James was going to see his boss about changing the timing of his holidays. He had made himself feel good beforehand by taking a few moments to breathe deeply and enjoy his cup of tea. He had then triggered himself into a relaxed yet alert state by remembering the last constructive encounter he had with the boss.

As he entered her office, his boss looked up at him and frowned. 'Oh no,' he thought to himself, 'she is in a bad mood, and won't want to know about my problems.' He immediately became apologetic and anxious. His whole demeanour made his boss wonder why he was so uncomfortable about his request, so she questioned it far more than she would normally have done.

Because our thoughts are so powerful, it is worth planning some of them to use for just such an occasion. If, as part of your preparation, you tell yourself some useful thoughts, they will help to maintain that appropriate state, and will stop there being space for the less useful ones to appear.

USEFUL THOUGHTS

Useful thoughts are those that help us to imagine the scenario going well. They remind us of:

- how we want to be in the encounter;
- how we want others to be;
- how we want the encounter to go.

EXAMPLES OF USEFUL THOUGHTS

'I want to be calm and decisive.'
'I will listen carefully.'
'He or she will be co-operative and helpful.'
'He or she will be interested in what I have to say.'
'We will have a useful discussion.'
'We will easily come to an agreement.'

Exercise 6 – Useful thoughts

What are some useful thoughts which you can come up with?
List a variety as a group, so you share each other's ideas.

Notice that this is a way of setting up our expectations, and we frequently get what we expect! By choosing to expect a positive and constructive encounter, and telling yourself so, you are far more likely to have just such an encounter.

BRINGING OUT THE BEST IN YOURSELF

All the techniques we have examined so far are ways of bringing out the best in yourself. They all help you to approach a situation in the right frame of mind to deal well with whatever it is.

To enhance this effect, it helps to remind yourself of other times when you have handled a similar situation well. We are our own best examples of how to be at our best, and all of us have useful experiences that we can call on.

We used this to create triggers – we took a time when you handled a situation well to help to identify how to be when you wanted to handle a situation you were less sure of.

Remind yourself of the many times when you have dealt with other people effectively. It doesn't matter what the circumstances were – the way you feel and act when it works well applies to any situation.

EXAMPLES MIGHT BE:
'I'm great with my teenage son, when he's being rebellious.'
'I can deal with irate customers well.'
'I always got on well with my colleagues at my last job.'

Exercise 7 – Dealing well with others

What are some of your examples of dealing well with other people? Use ones from home and social life as well as work. List at least four.

Replay specific experiences in your head, and just notice what you're like when you are handling the situation well; your posture, your facial expression, your tone of voice, your movements.

Remembering these experiences helps to remind you of your own unique way of being effective with other people, and sets you up automatically to adapt that effectiveness again. When you're unsure of your ground, use these memories to help yourself to feel more confident of your ability to handle the situation well.

BEING YOURSELF

In any situation, we are at our most effective when we allow ourselves to be true to ourselves. When we try to behave in ways that don't suit our personality, we come across to others as false, and are never comfortable enough to really be at our best.

It is important to acknowledge and appreciate your individuality, and work with your own strengths, so that it is the real you who is relating to others, not some pretender.

Scenario – Being yourself

Five new sales consultants were being trained in how to present and sell the product. They were taught a strict formula for achieving a sale, right down to what to say as a greeting to the potential client, and what facial expressions to have.

Simon knew that he could sell the product, but he also knew that the trained formula for doing so made him feel very uncomfortable. He played along with it in the initial training because he wanted the job, but when he tried it out with his first few clients, it felt stilted and he didn't make the sales.

The manager wasn't surprised. He had noticed that Simon wasn't comfortable with the formula, and suspected that he wouldn't make the grade.

But Simon wanted to succeed. He decided to try doing it his own way – after all, it couldn't bring any worse result.

His next client was surprised by his relaxed and rather light-hearted approach, but impressed by his obviously genuine belief in the product. He had a sale. In fact, he exceeded the first month's targets.

His manager reviewed with him, and asked him what had happened to turn him on to the formula. Simon just said that something must have clicked into place. That something was his individuality. His ambition now was to become a manager, because he believed he could train people so that he had an excellent team of individualized sales consultants. Only when he achieved that ambition did his 'secret' come out.

Exercise 8 – What makes you special?

What makes you special in the way you relate to people? Think of your good experiences with relating to others, and identify your particular strengths. Is it your sense of humour, your ability to listen, your knowledge, your kindness, your clarity? Identify your own list.

If you find this hard to do, imagine you are your own best friend. How would they describe what they like about you?

We have looked at how you can gain more control over your own moods and bring out the best in yourself, to prepare yourself for being effective with other people. It is useful to practise this self-management and to be encouraged by others to do so.

ACTION LIST – SELF-MANAGEMENT

As a group decide:

1. How you will help each other feel good.
2. If there are any negative triggers in your environment and what you can do about them.
3. How you can show appreciation of each other's individuality.

CHAPTER 3

BUILDING RAPPORT

KEY LEARNING POINTS

■ recognizing that good rapport is worth establishing
■ identifying the signs of good rapport
■ techniques to build rapport quickly
■ using rapport to improve a situation

NOTES TO MANAGER/COACH

I suggest that you read through this chapter first, to familiarize yourself with the material. You could put the definition of rapport on a flip chart as your starting point for the session.

It makes it more personalized if you can think of your own examples, rather than always use the ones given, so you might like to identify places where an example is useful, and make a note of your own. It is a good idea to use examples where the people involved are not known to the group, so that they don't make personal judgements.

When you split them into smaller groups, try to make the groupings different each time. By doing this, they are building rapport with different work colleagues through doing the exercises, and you increase the value of the session.

You may decide to have the ideas they come up with reproduced for them to keep as reminders. If you decide to do this, make sure you have facilities to do so, check you can read all the lists, and do it as soon as possible after the session, while it is still fresh in their minds.

Remember that the most important thing you will do is demonstrate rapport skills in the way you deal with the group. They won't get the message if you are not in rapport with them, and that is more important than sticking absolutely to your script, or getting things in the right order.

HOW RAPPORT FITS IN

In the last session we examined ways of preparing yourself to be in the right state to deal well with other people. If they had done the same sort of preparation, we would all find rapport very easy. However, this is not usually the case, so we need to begin to look at how we set up the first steps in relating well with those we have to deal with.

Building rapport means establishing a good basis for the relationship and is vital if we want to be able to work well with others. Some people are naturally good at this, but all of us can improve our skills, once we realize what makes the difference.

WHY BOTHER?

When we have rapport with others we work with, it makes our working life less stressful. If you get on with your work colleagues, there are fewer conflict situations, and it is easier to resolve problems, because there is a spirit of co-operation.

Scenario – Rapport in action

There is a major panic in one section of the manufacturing process. A vital piece of machinery has stopped working, and is holding up the whole process. The team in that section, and the sections on either side, all rush to see if they can sort out the problem. There is no recrimination, in fact there is even some joking in the midst of the crisis. These people get on well together, and will help each other out when the need arises. There is rapport between them.

One of the main things that people pick up on in a work situation is the 'atmosphere'. Where there is a good atmosphere, people work more effectively, produce better work, and go home less exhausted. And the atmosphere is to a large extent created by the level of rapport between people.

MEANING OF RAPPORT

The word 'rapport' comes from the French word that means carrying something back. In other words, rapport is about actively making sure that you have some shared message that you both send and receive. You hear people say things like: 'We're on the same wavelength' or 'She thinks along the same lines as me' – these indicate rapport.

Exercise 9 – Results of good rapport

Ask the group to identify the results of good rapport in working relationships. Get as many as you can and write them on a flip chart. Accept all the answers you are given and write them up exactly as they are said. There is a checklist of common answers listed below which you can use to add to their list, or to give them an example to start them off. When you have a reasonable list, comment that, if rapport brings so many possible benefits, it's certainly worth looking at ways of enhancing it.

Typical common results of good rapport

Easier working relationships	More productive
Better atmosphere	Enjoy coming to work
Easier to deal with problems	Less conflict
Less stress	More fun at work
Feel more respected/valued	

FIRST IMPRESSIONS

There are people whom we meet for the first time, and immediately know that we will get on with them. This first impression of someone being likeable is not just a 'happy accident'. Without realizing it, we all tell other people all sorts of things about ourselves, and it is these unconscious messages that give the first impression.

COMMON MESSAGES WE GIVE

Stop and think about the way we respond, physically, and in the tone of our voice, to someone we are fond of. Smiles, friendly body posture, soft and warm tone of voice, welcoming words, are what we expect and what we offer. We don't think about it consciously, it happens automatically, and the only time we really notice their reaction is when it's *not* what we expect. Then we'll ask them what's wrong, even before they have said anything.

Contrast this scenario with the way we react to someone we dislike. If we just dislike them, we are likely to have a cold tone of voice, to move ourselves away from rather than towards them, and to have a hard-looking expression on our face. If we also fear them or distrust them, we are likely to have a distrustful tone of voice, a wary expression on our face, or a slightly submissive body posture.

These are extreme reactions, but we all develop our own repertoire of ways of unconsciously reacting to others, based on our assumption or evidence of what they're like. And quite a lot of our assumptions about others are based on how they react to us, unconsciously!

Scenario – They are bound to object

Michael was anxious about the team meeting with his staff. He wanted them to agree to some new arrangements for the approach to dealing with customers, but thought that they were likely to object.

He decided to go in 'with all guns blazing', to counteract his own anxiety. He stood at the top of the room, while the rest of the team sat at the table as usual. His face was set and in a harsh tone he declared: 'The work pattern is going to change in the following way . . . '. His staff reacted with even more hostility than he had expected.

In this example, Michael had spoilt any chance of building rapport with his staff, to help set up a mood where they were more willing to consider his plan. By standing apart from them, so that he was both distant and looking down on them, he literally and emotionally distanced himself from them. His set face and harsh tone added the aggressive element, as did his decision to go in 'with all guns blazing', which gave him an aggressive body posture.

Consequently, psychologically they reacted by de-fending their present position, and responded to what they felt as hostility with hostility. Michael had created just what he wanted to avoid.

Scenario – We will get on

Dave was a newly appointed manager of a customer service team. The team had worked well with their previous manager, and resented a new boss.

Dave sensed the hostility but chose not to react to it. He smiled at everyone he met up with, he stayed relaxed and comfortable in his posture, he spoke clearly and yet with an easy tone of voice. And the team began to comment on the fact that he was a nice bloke, and began to react to him more positively.

What unconsciously affects our reactions to others is the manner in which they present themselves. In the two scenarios given, it is the manager's manner that provokes the differing responses.

So, to build good rapport with others, we need to

identify what the elements are of the manner that provokes a positive reaction, so that we can consciously choose to set ourselves up to be like that.

Exercise 10 – Features of someone who is easy to get on with

Talk to each other in pairs or threes about specific situations where you have found it easy to get on with someone, and identify: what the person's body posture was like, what their facial expression was like, what sort of things they said, and what tone of voice they used.

Feedback in the whole group the common features of someone who is easy to get on with, and record them on a flip chart. A typical list is featured below. The conclusion from the list you've produced is that if you can be like that as a first impression, then people will be more likely to find you easy to get on with.

Building rapport

Common features of someone who is easy to get on with may include:

They smile
They have a friendly tone of voice
They look at you
They say 'hello' when you pass them by
They look relaxed
They don't snap at you
They talk in a way you can understand
They act like a reasonable human being
They are friendly
They turn towards you
They remember things about you
They stop what they are doing and turn to listen to you
They pass the time of day, and don't just talk business

CHOOSING THE FIRST IMPRESSION WE GIVE

Once you realize that you play a part, albeit unconsciously, in setting up someone else's reaction to you, then you can consider what message you want to send, and take some control over those automatic reactions.

Just by slightly changing your body posture, relaxing

your jaw and forehead, and making your voice sound more gentle, you can significantly change the reaction of someone towards you. If you don't find it easy to make this sort of physical change, you can 'trick' yourself into it, by imagining that the person in front of you is someone you know, whom you like and respect. As soon as you do that, you will automatically change your body posture, voice tone, and facial expression.

This very simple technique gives you some control over the first impression you give to someone else, and can help you to begin to build useful rapport, because if you look as if you like and respect the person, they are more likely to respond to you automatically as someone to like and respect.

Exercise 11 – Establishing rapport

Practise making small adjustments to create the possibility of rapport. This means slightly changing body posture, facial expression, or voice tone. Make this fun, rather than hard work, but really do it, and say hello to each other, in pairs or threes, in the right way, correcting each other if necessary.

BEING GENUINE

Some people, who have learnt this technique, use it to try to create a first impression that is not genuine for them. The stereotypical salesperson is an example of this.

Scenario – A false front

You are considering double glazing your home. You can see the salesperson walking towards the front door, looking cold and fed up. He rings the doorbell, and, when you answer, he has a big forced smile on his face and greets you enthusiastically. Once seated, he proceeds to express great interest in your collection of CDs, claiming that he likes just the same music as you.

He then launches into his sales patter, totally disregarding your questions and concerns. You feel 'conned' even if the double glazing is really a reasonable deal, because you have not felt drawn towards the person.

It is important to remember that we do usually spot the difference between a false and a genuine reaction to us. The person giving a false impression of being friendly has consciously controlled some of their automatic reactions, but if they don't really mean it, there will be some signal that it is a false front, and we will pick it up. We talk about forced smiles and voices that are just a bit too loud – these are signs that someone is not genuine, and we are rightly wary.

WHAT IF YOU DON'T LIKE OR RESPECT THEM?
In working relationships, we sometimes need to establish rapport with people whom we would avoid in our personal lives.

To be able to give a positive first impression genuinely we need to think beyond the personality of the individual, and remind ourselves of the purpose of the interaction. For example, you may need a useful and constructive response from someone about an issue you have. If you concentrate on the fact that you want a useful and constructive response, rather than on your dislike of the person, you will be more likely to give the unconscious message that you expect that sort of response, rather than the message that you don't like the person.

When we encounter someone on a casual basis, for example, someone who is selling us a rail ticket, our initial expectation tends to be that they will respond constructively to us, and they usually do. Personality only clouds the issue once we have got to know the person, or when we do not get the response we want.

When we concentrate on the result that we want to achieve with the person, we are more likely to elicit from them their desire for the same result. Even if two people who work together don't like each other at all, they are both likely to want to make their own lives easier, avoid conflict, and get the jobs done effectively. By concentrating on these shared outcomes, they can establish enough genuine rapport to work effectively together without getting caught up in personal dislike. It is also worth noting that sometimes this also results in a revised opinion of each other, and improves the personal part of the relationship.

Scenario – Using rapport at work

Sarah was asked by her manager to take on a joint project with Brenda. Her first reaction was to want to refuse. Brenda came across as a spoilt young lady, who thought she was better than the others on the team because she was a graduate.

But the project was an interesting one, and would contribute to Sarah's career development. There was also no doubt that Brenda would be good at the technical part of the project. She decided to accept the project and arranged to meet with Brenda about it. At the meeting, she suggested that the way they could do this project effectively would be to identify what they could each bring to it, and what they would gain from doing it. They both felt that it was career development for them, and that they would enjoy the challenge.

Brenda stated that she would like to do the technical parts – and added, quietly, that she was less sure of the aspect that required interviewing people. Sarah began to feel a little more comfortable with her – maybe she wasn't as condescending as she had seemed.

RAPPORT IN PHYSICAL POSITIONING

We all know that it is difficult to establish rapport when we are awkwardly placed in position to someone else. The commonly recognized example is that of someone sitting themselves higher than you, and behind a desk, to intimidate you.

By consciously thinking about how you are positioned in relation to the other person, you can enhance the rapport between you. Removing physical barriers, sitting or standing side by side rather than opposite each other, and making the distance between you comfortable for both of you, will all make it easier to establish some rapport.

RAPPORT THROUGH LANGUAGE

There are some people we find it easy to talk to, because they 'speak the same language'. This need not be an accidental occurrence. By listening to how someone expresses themselves, we can learn the sort of expressions or language they prefer, and use that same type of format to get our message across. When you use someone else's way of saying something, they feel understood – unless you are mocking them – and they respond to you more.

You would probably recognize yourself that sometimes it grates when someone 'translates' what you say into their own words. For example, if you were to say, 'I want to get this job finished today' and someone said, 'So you're anxious to complete the task', it might mean that to them, but you're not anxious at all! If they say, 'So, how can I help you to get this job finished?', you would feel much more comfortable.

RAPPORT THROUGH COMMON GROUND

It is often stressed, in describing rapport, that you need to find common ground with the other person. This is sometimes an extra stress, as you keep trying to find something that you're both interested in, and keep discovering how different you are! And it's no good pretending you're interested in something that matters to them. If you're not genuine, it shows through, and can reduce rapport rather than build it.

However, it is quite easy to find common ground if you remember that you're relating to another human being. Most of us get up in the morning, have meals, enjoy sunshine, care about our children, etc. Just simple everyday human experiences are often the most effective common ground we have, and sharing humanness is more useful in building genuine rapport than anything else.

Often, people build rapport on this basis by very simple behaviours that are casual encounters, so that when they come to have a more in-depth interaction with that person, the rapport is already established. For example, saying hello and smiling at people as you pass in the corridor can have a significant effect on how they deal with you when you are in a prolonged meeting with them.

It is also worth remembering that both of you may want to do the job better, get the job done, resolve the issue, or make your working lives easier, and these shared intentions provide common ground in any interaction.

Exercise 12 – Finding a way of establishing rapport

Start by rearranging your chairs so that you feel really comfortable. Then chat to each other about your everyday lives, taking care to not 'translate' what each other says, but use the same type of language, and notice how you find common ground. We have looked at the effect of physical positioning, using the same type of language, and finding common ground. Now work in pairs or threes, so that you can explore ways of increasing rapport. Talk as a whole group about what you noticed.

DEALING WITH PROBLEM SITUATIONS

All we have looked at so far is common sense, and it happens automatically with people that we already get on with. The problem arises when there is someone whom you're not sure of, or haven't got immediate rapport with. When that happens, it is useful to know ways of improving the situation, for all the reasons we listed at the beginning of the session.

Scenario – Finding rapport

Peter had been told he was to have a coaching lesson with me. He was not pleased to find out that I was a relatively young female, who wasn't an engineer. His manner when he came in was very surly, and he made it clear that he didn't expect any benefit from the session.

I stayed relaxed, smiled at him, and suggested we had a cup of tea. He commented that he thought I would drink coffee, and we discussed the relative merits of different brands of tea, agreeing that the tea from the machine was lousy!

He started to relax, and I suggested that we sat in the more comfortable seats in the lounge, side by side. He then asked me if I knew anything about engineering. I laughed and said not as much as him, but some, because my dad was an engineer. He began to talk more freely, and the coaching session went well.

Exercise 13 – Improving rapport

Form small discussion groups, and come up with ways of improving the situation when you don't have much rapport with someone.

(It is useful if you pose specific problems to the group, for example: What do I do if someone is acting superior to me? What do I do if someone won't discuss something with me? Then the group are to come up with as many ideas as they can to solve the problem).

Ask them to record all the ideas they have. Feedback the ideas to the whole group, so that they share the common wisdom.

We have looked at simple ways of building rapport. Because it can make our working relationships more constructive and more enjoyable, it is worth spending the few moments it takes consciously to choose to make the small differences that will help us to establish rapport.

ACTION LIST – BUILDING RAPPORT

1. As a group, agree to check out your physical positioning and your manner, before you start talking to each other, and to adjust them to improve rapport if necessary.
2. Notice where you have instant rapport with someone and identify what they or you did that made the difference.
3. At the next encounter you have with someone where there isn't good rapport, experiment with changing your physical position, relaxing your posture, smiling, softening your voice tone, and see what happens.
4. See what common ground you can find with someone you think is very different from you.

CHAPTER 4

GIVING ATTENTION

KEY LEARNING POINTS

- realizing how giving attention is more than just listening
- being able to switch on full attention
- noticing the full information about how someone is
- using what you learn from giving attention

NOTES TO MANAGER/COACH

This session will give everyone the opportunity to learn how to give attention more effectively. It is important that you are a model of the theme, so make sure that you pay careful attention to your team during this session, and respond to any signals that require it. The demonstration of these different skills is a more powerful way of encouraging others to use them than just talking about it.

INTRODUCTION

In the last session, we looked at simple ways of building rapport with others, so that any encounter starts off on a better footing. Now we're going to examine how you can enhance any relationship further by giving the other person full attention.

WHAT IS ATTENTION?

We often think that we've given someone our full attention because we can repeat everything they said, verbatim. You see this ability to repeat used to deny the charge from a loved one that we weren't paying them attention: 'I heard everything you said. You were telling me that you wanted to get more exercise, and talking about ways of doing that.'

But I'm afraid that they were probably right to accuse you of not paying attention. Listening to the words and being able to repeat them is the lowest form of attention, not the highest. When we say people are good listeners, we mean much more than this.

When someone is really paying attention to us, we feel not just that they have listened, but that they have understood where we're coming from and what we really mean. The whole person is there for us, and is taking on our perspective on things rather than judging us.

We have to pay this level of attention to small babies, because there is no communication through language, and many parents are excellent at 'second-guessing' what their baby needs or wants. Once we start to speak, it is less common to receive this level of attention, and feel really understood by the other person.

Exercise 14 – Being paid full attention

Think of times when someone has paid you full attention. It may be a parent, a colleague, a friend or even a relative stranger.

In twos or threes, discuss what it felt like to receive someone's full attention, and what you thought of the person as a result. Feedback the main points to the whole group.

THE BENEFITS OF GIVING ATTENTION

You have identified some of the benefits of giving attention in Exercise 14. People tend to feel valued and taken notice of when they are given attention. They also have regard for the person concerned, and value their opinion more highly. No doubt you came up with other points.

There are more benefits to giving attention to others, besides the fact that it makes them feel important, and they value you more.

Scenario – Words at face value

Terry asked John if he would mind writing up a brief report on the project he had just completed, to present at the next team meeting.

John's reply was, 'I suppose not'. The words were said in an offhand way, and John's whole manner said that he wasn't keen to do it. But Terry chose to ignore that, and said, 'So you'll do it', and John said, 'Yes', reluctantly.

At the team meeting , when asked for his report, John said that he was sorry, but he hadn't had time to put it together. Terry confided to a colleague afterwards that he wasn't really surprised, because he had thought that John didn't really want to do it.

If Terry had given John full attention at the time, and picked up on his reluctance, he could have avoided this incident completely. If he had paid attention, he would have been able to ask John what the problem was. He then would have discovered that the work which John's colleague was supposed to take off him while the project was being done had not been done, so John was trying to catch up, so as not to get his colleague into trouble. He was feeling under pressure and resentful.

Instead, Terry assumed that John was being negative, and

only found out what had really been going on when he later challenged John about the incident. There was bad feeling all round, and it took a while for their relationship to improve.

Exercise 15 – Benefits of giving attention

From reviewing this example, list some of the other benefits of giving attention as a whole group. Add to this any more benefits you can think of.

HOW TO SWITCH ON FULL ATTENTION

There is no doubt that giving someone full attention is very useful, and has pay-offs for both them and you. In order to do this, we need to retrain ourselves, because most of the time we have only given first level attention, that is, we have at best just listened carefully to their words.

Most children, however, are very good at giving full attention, and we have all been children, so we just need to consciously relearn or remember the skill. Children are not conned by the mother who says, 'I'm fine', when she's really feeling angry about something. They use all their senses to deduce the state of someone, and are remarkably accurate and perceptive.

To do this requires switching on five levels of attention:

1. *Listening with your ears*   The first level, that picks up the words someone is saying – our normal level of attention.
2. *Listening with our inner ear*   Where we pick up the tone of voice, the meaning behind the words, the emphases and hesitations.
3. *Attending with your eyes*   Noticing how the person's body language supports or negates what they are saying, and where it's saying something entirely different.
4. *Attending with your guts*   This is the 'I knew, somehow' level, where our intuition is at work, and we get a sense of something, although it's not obviously being communicated.

5. *Attending with your heart*   Where we view the person sympathetically rather than judgementally, and get a sense of what it's like from their point of view.

This sounds complicated, but it's actually something we all do automatically sometimes. You may have given this level of attention when:

- you meet someone you find attractive, and want to find out more about them, to see if you want to take the relationship further;
- a family member or friend is in distress, and you want to help and show you care;
- you are not sure if the person is someone you can trust, and you need them to be trustworthy.

Exercise 16 – Switching on full attention

Practise consciously switching on full attention.

Begin by remembering a time when you have given your full attention to someone, and notice how you were: your body posture and level of relaxation; your facial expression; what went on in your head. (If you really can't think of an example, imagine how you would be if you were paying full attention to someone.)

Now, working in pairs, get ready to tell each other about an interesting event in your life. It can be anything from a recent event to something in your childhood.

You should take it in turns to tell your story, for about five minutes. The other person will just give attention, and not say anything. Before you begin the exercise as the person paying attention, remind yourself how you were when you gave attention before, and get into a similar posture, etc. You will then say to yourself, 'I am now switching on the five levels of attention'. Now, relax and enjoy just giving attention to the other person as they tell the story.

At the end of the exercise, let each person in the pair tell the other one something they realized about them as they were paying attention, for example:

'I realized that you're really involved in being a father.'
'I realized that you love adventure.'
'I realized that you're kind.'

Whenever you want to switch on full attention from now on, you just have to go through the two steps I suggested in the exercise:

1. Remember times when you've done it before, and how you were physically and mentally.
2. Tell yourself: 'I am now switching on the five levels of attention.'

You will be astonished by how much more you find out about people by using this simple technique. Just as when you were a child, you can become again accurate and perceptive in your observations.

APPLYING YOUR SKILLS IN ATTENTION

Once you start practising giving full attention, you will find lots of situations where it is useful. It is not, however, necessary to always give this much attention. In fact, we would go mad if we did, because we would be bombarded with information constantly from other people – some of which we would rather not know! The whole point of learning how to give attention consciously, is to be able to choose to use the skill when it's beneficial to you, and to the other person.

AT THE BEGINNING

I would suggest that it is **always** useful to pay full attention at the beginning of an encounter with someone. It is the most efficient way to find out what state they are in, so that you can adjust your behaviour to suit the situation.

Scenario – What state is she in?

Jeremy is really excited about some news he has just received concerning a project he is working on. He wants to tell his co-worker on the project, Susan, about it. Susan has just been to a meeting about the project where the response was fairly negative. On top of the fact that she slept badly last night and the anxiety she has about finding time to work on the project when her normal work-load seems to be increasing, this is just more than she can cope with.

Jeremy rushes up to her and blurts out his news. Her reaction is not what he expected. She is not convinced it will make any difference, and shows it. Then she tells him that the meeting went badly. He walks away disappointed, and beginning to feel less positive himself.

In this scenario, Jeremy's lack of attention in the beginning leads to a negative result for both of them. He has the wind taken out of his sails, and Susan doesn't have the positive effects of some good news. If he had paid attention to her in the beginning, he would have been able to handle it differently.

Scenario – What state is she in? Version 2

Jeremy goes to sit by Susan, and asks her how the meeting went. While she is telling him, he gives her his full attention. He notices that she is really feeling 'down' about it, and also senses that there's more to it than just the meeting.

When he speaks, he uses a gentle tone of voice, and asks her if it's just the meeting that's got her down. She then tells him what else is affecting her.

Now he introduces his news in a different way. He agrees that it's difficult to stay positive about the project when you have those sorts of reactions to it in a meeting, and when other work is mounting up, but says that he has just been encouraged to keep going by the news he has received.

Susan now listens with interest, and agrees that it's exciting. In fact, she clearly cheers up a bit.

> As he's about to leave, Jeremy suggests that they talk further the next morning about the pressures with the project. Susan smiles and says she'd like that. She agrees that she's sure that they can overcome the problems, and thinks that she'll feel better after a good night's sleep.

Can it really be so different? Oh yes! This is not an exaggerated example of the difference that attention can make, but an everyday one.

By paying attention, you can quickly ascertain whether someone is 'ready' for a positive meeting or not. If not, you can adjust your behaviour, to help to change their state. The very act of paying attention to them often effects a change – we all respond positively to being taken notice of.

Exercise 17 – Paying attention at the beginning of an interaction

Discuss a couple of your own examples of when paying attention at the beginning would have improved the situation. You may use work or domestic examples for this. You may like to do this in twos or threes.

DURING AN INTERACTION

As well as being useful to give attention at the beginning, so as to find out what someone is like before you start, it is also useful at different points in an interaction.

By paying attention when someone responds to you, you can establish a better understanding of what they are communicating. Their body language, their voice tone, their facial expression, will help you to know the importance of the response, its genuineness, and where you might need to find out more.

Scenario – Noticing someone's reaction

I was working with a group of mixed nationality. Someone came up to me and asked me if she could speak privately with me. I said of course, and we were just about to move to a quiet area when someone else of a different nationality came up and asked me a question. I asked him if he could wait a little while as I was already engaged with Hannah. Hannah blushed and said, 'It doesn't matter'. Everything about her manner said it **did** matter, so I insisted. She said during our conversation that she was glad I had insisted, but surprised. And what she wanted to talk about **was** important.

Exercise 18 – Paying attention during an interaction

Discuss when you think it would be important to pay attention during an interaction. Think of some examples that are likely to occur during your working week. Talk about them as a whole group, and give your reasons for saying your examples are important.

Do make sure that you pay each other attention as you make your points, rather than judging the points made.

WHY ATTENTION MATTERS

Why have I devoted a whole chapter to the subject of paying attention? Because it is one of the most important qualities to develop if you want to improve your people skills. It enhances significantly your rapport with others, because we all appreciate being paid full attention.

At the same time, it increases your awareness of the other person and how they are. This enables you to adjust the way in which you behave and communicate with them, so as to make the interaction more effective.

USING WHAT YOU LEARN FROM PAYING ATTENTION

In each of the scenarios where the person **was** paying attention, they have used the additional information gleaned to adjust their own approach.

By making adjustments that show consideration of the other person, you will enhance the relationship. This doesn't mean that you always 'fit in' with them, but it does mean that you demonstrate respect for their state.

You also gain, in that you are likely to get across what you want to communicate far more effectively as a result. It is not enough to tell someone something, we want to make sure that we have been taken notice of. By adjusting the way we present our case to suit how they are, we increase the likelihood of that happening.

CHANGING THE MOOD OF SOMEONE

Sometimes, however, it is worth taking some action to **change** the other person's state before attempting to get your message across.

Scenario – Changing someone's state

Carol wanted to talk to Steve about the customer she had taken over from him. She looked across at him and noticed that he looked quite angry. 'How's it going?' she asked. He snapped back that he never wanted to speak to another customer again. Not a good time to ask for constructive information about a customer!

Carol waited a few moments, then asked if he'd like her to fetch him a cup of coffee. He thanked her, and she brought it back, with one for herself, and went and sat by him. Casually she said, 'Do you remember when we worked together on the account with Jay's Fruit Stores last year? I was just thinking about the fun we had with that.' Steve, of course, did remember, and they began to talk about the delightful characters involved, and the sense of achievement they had with the project, because it was a tough one. After a while, it was clear that Steve was feeling more positive. In fact, he said, 'Maybe customers aren't so bad after all!' Now Carol could ask him about her new customer and get a useful response.

By distracting Steve from his negative mood, and reminding him of times when he felt good about working with customers, Carol helped Steve to feel more positive, but also made it much easier for herself to get the kind of response that she wanted. It only takes a short while to do this, and it's certainly worth while.

There are lots of ways of helping someone to change from a negative type of mood to a positive mood, and we have all found ways sometimes. For example, if you want to have a pleasant evening out with your partner, and they are not in a good mood, what do you do?

Exercise 19 – Ways of changing someone's mood

As a whole group, put together a list of possible ways you could change someone's mood from negative to positive. Think of the times when you've done it for someone else, or someone has helped you to change your mood. What are the tricks? Think of as many as possible, so that you have a repertoire of strategies ready for when you need them.

Examples might be:

Tell them a funny story
Give them a hug
Make them a cup of tea

DON'T ASSUME

Obviously, you don't only discover that someone is in a bad mood if you pay attention. You may discover that they are far more receptive than you expected, or you may discover that they have more of a sense of humour than you thought. Often, we assume that people are in a worse state than they are, especially if we have encountered them in a bad mood before, or if we've been told that they are difficult to deal with.

Paying attention gives us current information about someone and how they are, rather than basing the judgement on assumptions and prejudices.

CHECKING OUT YOUR INTERPRETATION

Of course, sometimes we make assumptions about the current information we're getting from someone. For example, we may see someone frowning and think, 'Oh no, they don't approve'. It is worth checking out whether we're picking up the message accurately. After all, they may just be concentrating.

A simple statement like: 'I notice you're frowning. Does that mean that you don't like that idea?' will elicit a clear answer from the other person. Sometimes you may not be able to make sense at all of what they are communicating, particularly when their words and their body language don't tell the same story. In this case, it is worth asking them to tell you what's going on: 'It seems to me that you're saying you want to do this, but you look like you would rather avoid it. Can you clarify for me?'

Most people appreciate you showing that you really want to understand their position, and respond well to your checking out. Occasionally they will be surprised, because they didn't realize that they weren't giving a clear message. And once in a while someone will react negatively to your checking out, because they didn't want you to notice – but it's worth risking the odd negative reaction for the benefits of the positive ones.

CONCLUSION

When we are interacting with others, we spend a lot of our time paying attention to our own concerns:

- do they like me;
- are they listening to me;
- how do I put this across;
- how long will this take;
- how am I going to do this.

This means that we are not noticing what state the other person is in, or how they are reacting. If we can suspend our usual egotistical approach to others for just a little while, both we and they gain a lot from the change to paying attention to them. They feel understood and listened to, and like you better for it. You have more useful information to help you make the encounter a good one.

ACTION LIST – GIVING ATTENTION

1. In your next encounter, pay attention to how the person is before you launch in.
2. Next time you're not sure what's going on with someone, ask them.
3. Notice people you meet who are good at paying attention, and compliment them on it.
4. Agree as a group to challenge each other when you don't think you're paying attention.

CHAPTER 5

RECOGNIZING AND WORKING WITH DIFFERENCES

KEY LEARNING POINTS

- learning from differences
- appreciating just how different we all are
- finding out about what matters to someone else
- gearing your message to the receiver
- using differences in a team

NOTES TO MANAGER/COACH

Even within your group, there will be some noticeable differences in personality and approach. Some will be quieter than others, some more cynical, some more willing to take risks, and so on.

It is important to demonstrate the value of differences while running the session, and to show genuine appreciation for what all the different perspectives have to offer. In particular, make sure you set the right tone for Exercise 20. It can help if you come up with some fairly outrageous examples of your own, and then ask people to celebrate!

INTRODUCTION

In the last chapter, we were examining the topic of paying attention. As you increase the level to which you give attention, you will notice in how many ways people are different from each other.

For one person, politeness is crucial, for another it matters more to get straight down to the core issue. For one person, time is the issue, for another, quality.

We all have our own priorities and core values, and they give us different ways of approaching things. The implication of this is that if you want to be skilful in dealing with other people, you have to learn to recognize and work with their differences.

NORMAL ATTITUDE TO DIFFERENCE

Most of us have not been brought up to value other people for their difference, anything but! We have learnt to judge others for their differences: 'He's better/worse than me, right/wrong, good/bad.' These judgements are not made by some independent code of conduct, they are made by comparison to what we have as our own priorities and values. It's no wonder that there are wars and smaller conflicts where both sides believe that they are right – from their own perspective, they are!

When we talk about valuing difference, we are talking about changing quite fundamentally our learned attitude to difference, and it requires some conscious effort.

LEARNING FROM DIFFERENCE

One of the ways we can make it easier to change this attitude is by realizing the benefits of appreciating differences in others. As children we knew these intuitively, and most small children do recognize and work with differences, until they learn not to by observing adults!

The first main benefit of difference is that it gives you the possibility of learning something new. Children are excited by difference because of this. They love going to new places, meeting new people, trying new activities. If, as adults, we take this same view of difference, we have the opportunity to broaden our horizons, increase our awareness of what is possible.

Scenario – Learning from differences

Geoff and Paul worked in the same office, and knew each other on a superficial level. They both knew that they weren't the same type, and made no effort to become better acquainted.

Geoff was very active and outgoing. He loved any sporting activity, and he was the one who livened up the office, making jokes, telling stories, and so on. Paul, on the other hand, was very quiet. He did his job well, but pretty much kept himself to himself. One or two of their colleagues had discovered that he was a kind and sympathetic listener when they were finding things tough, but most knew little about him.

Geoff and Paul were put together in a training exercise to value differences. It was difficult to get them to come back to the group, as they had become fascinated by each other's very different lifestyles and approaches.

Several months later, Geoff was talking about how much he was benefiting from his yoga classes. Others laughed and said that they wouldn't have expected him to do yoga. He said that he had Paul to thank for introducing him to something different. Paul laughed, and said that he also had learnt something new – he now really enjoyed going to football matches! Everyone was amazed that two such different characters had found activities they both liked.

This is a delightful example of what happens when people begin to appreciate and learn from difference. Not only did Geoff and Paul get involved in different activities as a result of their contact, they also began to 'open up' in other ways. Geoff became calmer and more able to listen to others and Paul became more assertive in the team, offering his opinions in team meetings and contributing more to general discussions. They both learnt and gained from exploring their differences.

If we weren't different from each other, we would be very boring! Most of us are tempted into extending our horizons because we come across examples of others who have already done so. By actively searching out those examples, we can increase our learning and development considerably.

However, what we do more commonly is look for people who are the same as us, or ways in which they are similar, because then we feel safe. This is such an ingrained habit that it requires a conscious effort to do the opposite.

Exercise 20 – Celebrating differences

In this activity you will be celebrating difference.

It's a chance to practise consciously finding the differences between you and others, and delighting in them rather than judging, and you can have some fun doing this activity.

The task is to find something different about yourself from any other person in the group. These differences will be in three ways, so there are three rounds to the activity:

1. *Difference in things you have*   An easy one this. What possessions do you have that no one else in the group has? It might be types of furniture, objects, clothing, etc.
2. *Difference in your habits*   What do you do that no one else does? It might be where you put your dirty clothes, how you clean your teeth, what your morning/evening rituals are, etc.
3. *Difference in your hobbies and interests*   What do you enjoy as an activity that no one else does? It might be African dance, skiing, yoga, stamp collecting, etc.

If someone says something that others share, it doesn't count, and you have succeeded when everyone in the group has expressed something different for each round. In fact, you are to celebrate by cheering or applauding yourselves!

It is very important to keep from judging in this activity. If someone says that they enjoy cutting photos of snails out of magazines, your response is, 'How wonderful! I don't do that!' rather than, 'What on earth for?' or 'How stupid!'

USING YOUR AWARENESS OF DIFFERENCE

By finding out how others are different from us, we gain very useful information for helping us to deal with them more effectively. It enables us to understand better a different perspective on issues, and also to appeal more to that person's perspective.

We don't just learn about different lifestyles, habits and interests when we pay attention to differences. We also learn about different views, different values, and different ways of thinking about and tackling things. This helps us to extend our repertoire, and encourages us to learn how to cater for those differences.

Scenario – Working with different people

I was to work on a project with Terry. He and I were both known for turning out good work, and we had been asked to work together.

At our first meeting, I stood by the flip chart and said, 'OK, where shall we start?' He walked round and round the room, then came to the flip chart and began drawing a flow-chart diagram.

At first I found this quite disruptive. I thought his walking was impatience or lack of attention, and his takeover of the flip chart with a diagram instead of a list irritated me. Then I was fascinated by the apparent difference in our approaches, and asked him to describe to me how exactly he went about doing a project. I then told him what my process was. We both liked the idea of parts of the other's approach, and decided to try out a synthesized version, while keeping in the parts that we felt we couldn't do without.

It meant that some things were in one sense duplicated — for example, he had a flow chart of the process, while I started with a list of the main elements to be covered — similar material in different forms. But we found that different things came out through our different approaches and enriched what we were doing.

And I really began to like the idea of walking around to get the ideas flowing, instead of finding his walking distracting.

The end-result was a good project, and a learning of new ways of approaching something for both of us. We could have ended up falling out, with both of us insisting that we knew the 'best' way of approaching a project. After all, we were both experienced and had good results from our own approaches. However, by exploring and experimenting with the differences between us, we were able to both cater for our individual preferences and learn from each other, so that we ended up with a process that worked effectively for us as a team, and both improved our individual approaches as well.

FINDING OUT ABOUT DIFFERENCES

It is not always obvious that someone has a different approach or perspective. We are used to trying to conform to the norm in our organizations or teams or lives in general, and will suppress our preferences to try to fit in. If you are going to use and learn from awareness of differences in others, you need to begin by finding out what those differences are.

To do this, it is useful to ask questions that will give you that information. We often ask questions when someone seems to be doing something or thinking differently from us.

Unfortunately the questions frequently seem judgemental, and provoke a defensive reaction rather than clear information.

Scenario – Causing defensiveness

Philip had just completed a piece of work with a customer and was reporting back to his manager. Although the work had been agreed beforehand, part way through Philip had decided to change the format of the final product. When he said this, his manager immediately leapt in and asked: 'Why on earth did you do that? We had agreed the format and you should have stuck to the original plan.'

Philip became defensive and said that he thought that the final result was better than the original concept. He didn't explain why, or even what had prompted him to make the decision. His manager told him that he was out of order, and not to do it again. Both ended up feeling disgruntled: Philip because he knew the customer was really pleased with the result, and he resented being told off for it; his manager because she had been involved in the original planning and preferred the original concept.

She later found out that the customer was delighted because Philip's alteration was a response to a request from the customer. She then had to talk to Philip again, and apologize for taking it wrongly. But she still felt cross because he hadn't explained to her properly in the first place.

If only this manager had asked Philip a different question! She could have asked: 'What prompted you to make that decision?' and would have found out immediately that it was response to a customer's request.

When something is different from what we are expecting, we need to find out about it before we judge, rather than ask judgemental questions.

USEFUL QUESTIONS

Useful questions begin with 'What?' or 'How?'. Examples might be:

- How did you do that?
- What prompted you to handle it in that way?
- How did that help?
- What does that mean to you?
- How is that important for you?

If we want to find out more about what matters to someone, we might ask:

- What matters to you about this?
- What do you enjoy about your work?
- What gives you most satisfaction?
- If you were left to your own devices, how would you deal with this?

By finding out more about the way the individual thinks about things, and what matters to them, we gain information that we can use to ensure that we appeal to them when we communicate with them.

This doesn't need to be a deliberate interview of the other person. In fact, it is often more effective if you have just an informal conversation. Asking people to talk about themselves, their work, other things they're doing usually provides you with the subject matter. The questions can then be used to prompt the extra information you want.

Exercise 21 – Asking useful questions

Get into pairs, each one of you in turn to be the listener and the talker. Take five minutes per person.

Talker   Choose some event that has recently happened at work, and tell the person about it.

Listener Listen carefully to what the talker is telling you, and ask two or three of the useful questions to find out more. Remember to use what or how, not why.

Discuss as a whole group what you discovered by being the talker, and then what you discovered as listener.

GEARING YOUR MESSAGE TO THE RECEIVER

Once you have found out what really matters to the other person, you can make your communication with them much more effective.

APPEALING TO THEIR PREFERENCES

We all respond more positively to communication that seems relevant to us, or is expressed in ways that appeal to us.

Scenario – Appealing to the other person's preferences

My child wants me to go to the park with him on a rainy, cold afternoon. If I look at it from my perspective, I'll say: 'No, I don't want to get wet and cold, and that wouldn't be good for you either.' His response would be to plead with me and probably to sulk if the pleading didn't work.

If I think about what matters to him and what would appeal to him, I come up with a different response: 'Rather than go to the park today, let's see if we can make a castle out of your Lego bricks, and we'll go to the park when the sun is shining, so you can play on the swings and slide without getting a wet bottom!'

I know he likes playing with Lego, I know he wants me to be involved in his activity and I know he wants to go to the playground at the park. He is now likely to respond by fetching his Lego bricks, and I just have to remember that I've promised a visit to the park when the sun shines!

If we are at all sensible, as parents, we tend to take this sort of approach because it makes our life easier. The same thing applies to our interactions with other adults. By taking account of their preferences, their viewpoint on things in the way we communicate with them, we make life easier for ourselves, because we avoid resentment, misunderstandings or resistance.

To make your communication effective, you need to stop and consider it from the other's viewpoint:

- If I were them, what would make me want to do this?
- If I were them, what would make this seem relevant to me?
- If I were them, what would make this important for me?
- If I were them, what would make me take notice of this?
- If I were them, what would make me respond positively to this?

With your answers to these questions, which are supplied by finding out about their differences, you can make your communication fit the receiver.

Scenario – Catering for different perspectives

Judy wanted her colleagues to agree to supporting a charity by doing a sponsored walk one Saturday, as part of a national sponsored walk day. To make it more likely that she gained their agreement, she thought about what would catch the interest of each of them.

Supporting a charity for children in need would appeal to Clara and Jack, who both had young children of their own. Proving his own fitness would appeal to Syd, who was a keep-fit fanatic. Getting lots of sponsors would appeal to Mary, who was good at wheedling money out of people. Seeing it as a way of bringing the team together would appeal to Edna, the manager, who was always wanting them to share activities. Hazel would want to join in if Clara did, because they were good friends. That only left Mike, who disliked physical activity and wouldn't like giving up his Saturday. However, he would like the idea of a pub lunch at the end of the walk, and would see it as important if the boss said it was.

> She could now prepare what she said, so as to appeal to all of them and had clarified that she needed to talk to Edna first, and win her over, before bringing it up at the team meeting.

Exercise 22 − Catering for people's differences

Work in pairs. Choose something that you might want your colleague to do, e.g. help you find something, help you finish a job, read an article on something, etc. Think about their perspective on things, and then try out your communication.

Example

> John, I need to find out when the next health and safety trainings are. I know that you're good at keeping papers filed correctly, and probably have the information. You also believe that such training is important and I know you'd support me in wanting to do it. Can you help me?

Now ask your colleague for feedback about what you said: what worked with them, plus anything else that would have been useful.

Do the same again, reversing roles.

Feedback to the whole group what you found doing the activity.

By using information you have found out about them, to express your message in a way that appeals to the other person, you increase the likelihood of them taking notice of you.

USING THEIR LANGUAGE

Another simple way to use the information others give you is by noticing how they express things. Some people use complex vocabulary, and some express themselves in simple language. Everyone has favourite phrases or expressions, and every group or company has its own particular use of language, where often ordinary words have particular meanings.

If you pay attention to the way someone uses language, you can use similar language to communicate your message to them, and they will receive it more readily, just because it's already in their language.

This may sound silly, but it's an important point in our communication. Think for yourself of the effect on you when you tell someone that you're fed up about something, and they ask you what you've got a problem with. You haven't got a problem, you're fed up! And already you feel that they are not really listening to you.

Remember, too, times when someone has been talking to you, and you've thought, 'That just went over my head'. The expression implies that they weren't talking in language that made sense to you.

We all know that if we are in a country where people speak a different language, it is harder to make yourself understood unless you learn the language. We often forget that, even within a common language, there can be great variations in the way we use it. By bothering to notice and use their way of using the language, you can make communication much easier.

THE RIGHT APPROACH

Having found out about how people differ, you can make it easier for yourself to get your message across by approaching them in a way that will work for them.

- Some people respond to an informal approach, some prefer to be prepared and have the time booked in their diary.
- Some people are more likely to respond well in the morning, others are more responsive in the afternoon.
- Some people don't mind being interrupted if they're doing something, others dislike it intensely.
- Some people like the communication to be short and focused, others prefer it to be part of a more general conversation.

Exercise 23 – Expressing your preferred approach

Think about what you prefer as an approach if someone wants to tell you something. Look at the list above of possible preferences, and add any other preferences you can think of.

Then tell the rest of the group, in turn, what you prefer as an approach. Listen carefully to what the others say – this is very useful information!

MAKING USE OF THE DIFFERENCES IN A TEAM

Implicit in this exploration of differences in individuals is the suggestion that differences can be useful. One of the benefits of working in a team is that people are brought together to offer their different strengths and perspectives for the communal benefit. We would consider it downright stupid to construct a football team of players who were all good at defence. It is the mixture of skills, talents and abilities that makes a team a strong team.

When working with others, we need to bear in mind that their differences will bring the greatest benefit.

Scenario – Using differences in a team

Ruth was trying to sort out a problem a customer had highlighted. She had examined the procedure over and over again, but couldn't see what was going wrong. She went to Ben, who had, like her, been involved in devising the procedure, and asked him for help. She explained that she knew the procedure was not working, from the customer's complaint, but couldn't find where the problem was. She thought Ben could help, as he knew the procedure as well as she did. Ben suggested that she would be better asking Elaine for help.

'But Elaine doesn't know this procedure,' said Ruth.

'Exactly,' said Ben. 'Because she doesn't know it, she will see it with an objective perspective, and question things that you or I would take for granted. And Elaine is good at asking questions.'

We all tend to prefer to consult with 'someone like us'. However, they may not be the most useful person for us to consult. If we really want to gain from the contact, we may be better off talking to someone who has different strengths or a different perspective. Within any team, there are a variety of skills and qualities that all have their value to the team, if properly utilized by other members, as well as by the person themselves.

Exercise 24 – Your contribution to the team

Think of two things you can contribute to your team. They may be skills, such as knowledge of a software package or being good at fixing things. Or they may be qualities, such as being a good listener or being optimistic.

Tell the rest of the group the two things you think you contribute, in turn. As each person has their turn, other people in the group can add other things that they think that person contributes.

For example, I might say that I am good at spotting spelling mistakes and I'm good at coming up with imaginative ideas. Others may add that I'm good at being hospitable with visitors, I'm good at making people laugh and I'm good at making sure a job has been properly finished.

In this chapter, we have examined how recognizing and working with differences adds value both for us and for others in our working relationships. It requires conscious effort to shift from judging and valuing differences, but the pay-off makes the effort worth while.

ACTION LIST – RECOGNIZING AND WORKING WITH DIFFERENCES

1. You have found out about some of the ways in which others in your team are different from you. Find out about some more differences. Talk to one of your colleagues whom you don't know well, and find out about their differences.
2. Before giving information to two people in the next week, stop and ask yourself: 'If I were them, what would make me take notice of this?'
3. Notice how two people you have contact with express themselves, and use their language to get your message across to them.
4. Use the information you have about what people in the group prefer as an approach, and try it out.
5. Next time you're stuck on something, approach a colleague who has an appropriate strength to help you. Make it explicit that you're choosing them because they are different from you.

CHAPTER 6

CONVEYING YOUR MESSAGE CLEARLY

KEY LEARNING POINTS

- clarifying your intention for yourself
- checking that the message you give fits your intention
- rehearsing your message
- noticing response
- reviewing your communication
- remembering we are always giving messages

NOTES TO MANAGER/COACH

It is particularly important with this chapter that you read through and prepare yourself beforehand. You are giving a live example of presenting your message, so it needs to be a good example.

When you do Exercise 27, it would be helpful if you were to read the instructions out loud to the group, slowly, with gaps for them to rehearse in their imaginations. If you suggest that they close their eyes to do this, it will work better.

INTRODUCTION

In the last two chapters, we have been exploring the ways in which you can find out more about other people, so that you can make sure that your message or communication is geared to produce a positive response.

However, the effectiveness of your contact with others is based just as much on awareness of yourself as the message-giver. Whether we like it or not, we are our message, and the two cannot be separated. So we need to explore ways of ensuring that our message comes across clearly whenever we are in contact with other people.

WHAT DO I WANT TO CONVEY?

Usually when we ask ourselves this question, we think about the content of our message:

- 'I'll tell them about the new policy.'
- 'I'll ask him about the problem.'

Yet this is not the full extent of what we want to convey to others.

Whenever we have contact with other people, we are, often despite ourselves, conveying a whole series of messages besides the obvious content of our interaction. We are conveying to them:

- what sort of person we are;
- how we want to relate to them;
- what we think of them;
- how we feel about our overt message;
- how we operate in the world.

If you stop to consider this for a moment, you will realize that you have formed opinions about a person that relate to these different categories, even if your only contact with them is for very businesslike reasons. We decide if they are genuine, if they are pleasant, if they like us, if they mean what they say, within moments of contact.

I referred to this when I discussed the importance of first

impressions in Chapter 2. It goes further than that, however. We need to consider carefully what our intention is in communicating with this person, to ensure that we convey the message clearly.

WHAT IS YOUR MESSAGE INTENDED TO ACHIEVE?

When we communicate with someone, there is always some sort of purpose behind it. It may be:

- we want them to take some action;
- we want them to come to some decision;
- we want to ensure that they have some information;
- we want them to agree with something;
- we want to enhance the relationship;
- we want them to feel that we've taken notice of them;
- we want them to give us some information;
- we want them to appreciate us;
- we want them to know more about us.

It is vital for us to clarify beforehand which of these apply in this particular communication, so that we express ourselves in a way that meets our full purpose.

To make it easier to identify your purpose, you can think of what would make it feel successful from your point of view:

- What will they do as a result?
- How will they feel as a result?
- How will I feel as a result?
- What will be the longer–term effect?

Often, when we are thinking about a specific interaction with someone, we only consider the first point: what will they do as a result.

Scenario — The wrong sort of agreement

Mary was meeting with colleagues to discuss a project she had taken on. She wanted them to agree to lengthening the deadline on it as she was very busy. She had come up with a list of reasons why they should agree, making the point that she had been off work ill for a week, and that she was under pressure because she also had a conference to arrange, on top of her normal work-load.

She succeeded in getting their agreement, but she didn't feel good at the end of the meeting. She was right to feel concerned. Afterwards her colleagues discussed the situation and expressed their concern that she wasn't really committed to the project; they also felt that they were being morally blackmailed into agreeing to the extension of the deadline. She had got the result she wanted at a superficial level, but had reduced her colleagues' respect and trust of her in the process.

If Mary had thought through her intention and outcome properly, she would have communicated her message very differently:

I want them to agree to extending my deadline because I'm very busy. (What will they do as a result?)

I want them to recognize that I'm committed to doing a quality job, and so I need to emphasize that my reasons are linked to wanting to do it properly. I want them to feel that I've been straight with them, so I need to emphasize that I take responsibility for not being able to meet the deadline. I want them to feel comfortable with agreeing to the extension, so I need to be clear about when I will have finished, and make doing so a priority. (How will they feel as a result?)

I want to feel supported in my request and encouraged to do it well, so I need to make it clear that this is what I intend. (How will I feel as a result?)

I want to be trusted by my colleagues to do a job well,

and to be seen as someone who is honest. I also want to feel able to call on their help if I genuinely need it. (The longer-term effect.)

Just thinking through your intention and outcomes in this way, you significantly change the way you will communicate with others. It puts a different frame around what you are wanting to get across, and you will automatically adjust your communication accordingly.

Exercise 25 – Your intention and outcomes

Think of an interaction that you will have in the next few days. Write down brief notes about what you want to achieve through that interaction, using the four categories as a guide. Share your thoughts with one other person, and ask them if they notice anything you may have left out.

It takes much longer to write this down than it does just to think it through. The few moments spent clarifying your intention are time well spent, because you are now more likely to communicate in a way that works for you and for the other person.

CHECKING THAT THE MESSAGE FITS THE INTENTION

The next stage of preparing to communicate is to ensure that the message you give will match the intention you have. This may seem obvious, but we frequently don't do this check!

THE TONE OF THE VERBAL MESSAGE

We need to check first that our verbal message sounds right. This means thinking about the words you will say, the type of language you will use (see Chapter 4), and the emphasis you want to give to different points you want to make. Notice that clarifying your full intention and outcomes will help with this part.

You also need to think about the tone you will use. Will

you sound friendly, efficient, assertive, angry, professional, helpful? No doubt you can think of other adjectives that might describe the tone of your voice.

Don't underestimate the importance of sounding right. If someone says to me, 'Of course I'll do it!' in a sharp tone, I feel reprimanded for even asking, and take that feeling away with me, rather than being pleased that they have agreed.

THE REST OF YOUR MESSAGE

Remember that what you say and the tone you use are only part of your message. Your whole body conveys an additional and powerful part of the message. If you do not feel comfortable with what you are trying to convey, it shows clearly in your body language, and affects strongly what is received as communication from you.

Scenario – The body language

A well-known speaker in the business field was giving a talk at a conference I attended. A colleague was discussing his speech afterwards with me.

Me	What impressed you about his talk?
Colleague	He obviously knows what he's talking about.
Me	What makes you think that?
Colleague	Well, you just have to look at him. He's so sure of his ground, and he answers questions with such confidence.
Me	Maybe he's just used to speaking in public.
Colleague	No, you can tell he's genuine. Listen to the feeling in his voice, watch his face. He obviously cares about his subject.

Notice that nothing was said about the actual content of his speech. All the evidence my colleague cited for being impressed with this speaker was about his voice tone and his physical manner while speaking. This evidence is what makes us take notice of what's actually being said.

Exercise 26 – Non-verbal messages

Talk together about your own examples of people whose message you take notice of, because their non-verbal message fits with what they are saying. Notice and remark on what you use as evidence.

WHAT IF YOU'RE NOT COMFORTABLE?

There are two reasons for not being comfortable with your message.

One is that you haven't thought about your own physical state and tone of voice, so you haven't consciously adjusted them to fit the message. We often carry over the physical reaction to one situation into another, and don't consciously adjust it to suit the new situation.

You just need to take a breathing space, and consciously set yourself up physically and mentally to match your message (see Chapter 2).

The other reason, which it is important to recognize beforehand, is when you are genuinely not able to feel comfortable with the message. In this instance, however much you try to set yourself up to give the right impression, it will slip away, and you will unconsciously convey a mixed message. You therefore need to stop to reconsider your message. If it is not one you can feel comfortable with, you will convey your discomfort.

Scenario – What can I convey genuinely?

Danny has been reading about teamwork and it seemed to him that you had to like your fellow team members to work effectively as a team.

He didn't like Joe as a personality. Joe was very boisterous and always had an opinion on every subject.

Danny thought he was pushy and over-confident, and certainly wouldn't want him for a friend. They had never got on very well.

However, he thought he should try to act as if he liked Joe, so that they would work together better. When he considered how he could communicate to Joe that he liked him, he realized that he couldn't feel comfortable with it, and that he would probably worsen the relationship rather than improve it.

When he stopped and reconsidered, he realized that what he really wanted was that they could work more effectively together. This was a genuine desire, so he could be more comfortable in conveying that message in their communications.

REHEARSING THE MESSAGE

When people are going to give an important presentation they are usually advised to rehearse it first, so that they are comfortable with their material.

I would advise you to rehearse many more of your 'presentations', but in a simpler, quicker way. The method I propose is to use your imagination.

You start by running through the scene in your imagination, as you expect it to go. This is the starting point for the rehearsal. If it were a real rehearsal, you wouldn't expect this version to be the final version, you would expect to improve on it. While you can't change the way others react directly, you **can** change the way you are, and have an indirect effect on others' reactions.

What people usually concentrate on when rehearsing a presentation is getting the words right. In your imagination, you can check on more than just getting the words right, you can improve the whole performance.

Scenario – Rehearsing a scenario

I am going to meet with a colleague to discuss some work we are doing. What usually happens is that we start arguing because we approach things in a different way. She usually argues so hard that I end up giving in to her, just to finish the business, but I never feel as if she's listened to me, and sometimes my idea would have been better than hers.

I want to improve this scenario, so I begin to rehearse it in my imagination. To start with, I think about what I'm going to say. Usually I just launch in with my ideas, and then she argues against me. I try out, in my imagination, what would happen if I suggest that we both put our different ideas on the table, and then discuss the best way, and if I get her to go first. It seems to me that that would work better, but I realize that there's a danger of me shooting her ideas down in flames. I need to find a way of expressing my ideas that isn't a straight contradiction of hers. I have another try, banning myself from using the words, 'You're wrong'.

Now I listen to the way I speak to her. I usually sound defensive before we even start arguing! I remember that I speak in a different tone of voice to another colleague, whom I find easy to work with, and decide to use that tone of voice in this scenario. Again, I briefly rehearse it in my imagination, and feel that it will make a positive difference.

Finally, I step back in my imagination and look at my own physical positioning and facial expression. I usually sit down opposite her, and adopt quite a tense-looking position, and there's not a smile to be seen. I decide to try out sitting on the same side of the table as her, so we're side by side, and consciously relaxing my posture, so that I'm less tense. I might even try smiling!

These are all small changes, and quickly identified when I do my imaginary rehearsals. Yet they can significantly change what happens when I go into the real situation, as this example proves.

My colleague was delighted to be asked to put her ideas first, and said that she always felt that she had to defend her ideas vigorously because mine were put first, so I obviously thought they were the best ones. She also asked me what had put me in such a good mood – she was used to receiving the bad mood version of me. And we ended up agreeing much more quickly on an approach that used some of her ideas and quite a lot of mine.

We often do rehearse scenarios in our imaginations, but we usually imagine them going badly, and rarely recognize that we could change what happened by doing something different ourselves in the first place. This way of rehearsing helps us to improve our own performance, so as to be more effective in provoking a positive reaction from the other person.

Exercise 27 – Rehearsing a scenario

Individually, take a scenario that will be coming up for you in the near future – you may choose the same one as for Exercise 25, or a different one.

Start by imagining how it would usually go – your starting point. Now think about your intentions in this interaction, and how you would like it to go.

You know what you want to say, think about how you can express it in a way that will provoke a better reaction in the other person.

Now imagine the tone of your voice. Is it one that suggests a positive intention? Is it the same as you use in situations that are really comfortable for you? If not, imagine yourself speaking in that changed tone of voice, and imagine the difference it can make.

Finally, take a step back from the scene, in your imagination, as if you were director of this performance. Review how you, as actor, look physically and are positioned in relation to the other person. Does it convey the message you want to convey? If not, suggest some adjustments to yourself, and imagine how the scenario would go with all these improvements in place.

At the end of the exercise, just run through again, in your imagination, the improved version of the scenario, to set yourself up to make this version happen when you come to the real situation.

As a whole group, discuss anything that you realized while doing this exercise.

NOTICING THE RESPONSE

When we come to the point of conveying our message in the real situation, we are often so geared up to making sure we tell the other person whatever it is, that we forget to notice how they are responding until we have finished.

There is nothing more frustrating than having someone say, 'You lost me in the first sixty seconds, so can you repeat it?' It is important to monitor their response continually, so you can adjust your message to suit.

REASONS FOR A POOR RESPONSE

There is a myriad of reasons why someone may not receive your message as you intended, and most of them may not be directly related to you.

People come with their own baggage into a situation. You may have done preparation to clear yours, but they are likely to still have theirs with them! They may be thinking about what they've just been doing, or what they have to do next. They may just be tired, or in a bad mood. They may expect you to be awkward, so be set up to be defensive.

You cannot foresee every eventuality, but you can notice that the response is not how you want it to be, and do something about it.

CHANGING THE RESPONSE

There are three main ways of changing the other person's response, so that it matches with what you intended.

A DIFFERENT APPROACH

The first, and most obvious, is to try a different way of

conveying your message. Although this is obvious, many people don't do it – they repeat their message in exactly the same way, and expect it to get through the second or third time. This method is not effective if they have not understood what you mean. To convey it differently, try considering it from the other person's point of view:

- Is it in the right sort of language for them?
- Would they grasp it better if it were made visual in some way – a diagram, bullet points or a picture?
- Can you find an analogy for it, something they already know that you can relate it to, so you can begin by saying, 'It's like when you …'?

TIME TO RECOVER STATE

If the problem is not lack of understanding, but lack of interest, then you may need to consider whether they are in the right mood to allow you to convey your message. In this instance, you need to encourage them to change their attitude, either by tempting them into being interested, or by suggesting that they take the time they need to get into a more positive frame of mind.

You may want to ask yourself, 'What would make them feel that my message was important/relevant/interesting?' and adjust your message accordingly. Or you may ask them when would be a better time to talk to them, because you would like them to respond constructively.

THE DIRECT APPROACH

If you are still not getting through to someone, then you can try the third way of changing their response: you can ask them to tell you what would change their attitude. This is something we rarely think of doing – instead we continue to try to guess, becoming more and more uncomfortable as we do so, and therefore less able to convey our message well.

There are some simple questions we can ask that will usually give us the information we need.

- 'What would make it possible for you to respond constructively to my suggestion?'
- 'How can I interest you in this information?'
- 'What do you want to hear from me?'
- 'What would provoke a more positive response from you?'

By using this direct approach, we can find out from the person what would make the difference to them.

Scenario – The direct approach

I was asked to explain to a group what we would be doing in a forthcoming training programme. The purpose was to motivate them to want to be involved, rather than to feel forced into it.

I began to explain, but quickly sensed that they were not with me. I tried presenting the information diagrammatically, but that didn't make the difference.

I suggested we took a short break for them to have a cup of coffee, and hoped that it would give them a chance to find a more positive attitude.

They came back to the room in much the same frame of mind, so I started by asking them what would make them want to be involved in this training. I then discovered that no one had told them why the training had been agreed, and that they thought that it was because they had been identified as being useless in this particular skill area.

I was then able to explain to them that the purpose of the training was to produce some high-flyers in this area, and that they were seen as capable of being those high-flyers. Now they were ready to hear about the content.

Exercise 28 – Provoking a positive response

Think of a time when you didn't get the response you wanted from someone. Consider now what you could have done to provoke a more positive response.

Pair up with someone and talk about your examples.

REVIEWING YOUR COMMUNICATION

The exercise you have just done is part of what we can do to continually improve our own standards of communicating clearly.

It is not easy to get your message across clearly and effectively. None of us is perfect at it. However, we can continually improve the way in which we do it, by briefly reviewing our communications after the event.

We need to simply ask ourselves two questions:

1. *What did I do that worked well?* Review the parts that worked well, so that you remind yourself of useful techniques.
2. *What would I do differently next time?* Choose just one part that didn't provoke the response you wanted, and think of a different way of handling it.

The review takes only a moment or two, but it is very effective in prompting us into even better ways of getting our message across.

CONCLUSION

We are always conveying a message of some kind to everyone we have contact with, even if we don't speak to them, or we have nothing in particular we wish to convey.

It is really important to be aware that we are constantly communicating, and that simply switching on these techniques when you think it matters is not enough. The person that we want to listen to us positively will also have received messages from us about how we value them, and what we think of them when we passed them in the corridor or greeted them in the morning.

We need to constantly be aware of the attitude we are showing towards others, because they will respond to us according to our attitude as much as according to our overt message.

ACTION LIST – CONVEYING YOUR MESSAGE CLEARLY

1. For one situation in the next week, stop and think about your intention and outcomes, and rehearse the scenario in your imagination, making improvements.
2. When you don't get the response you want in a situation, experiment with asking the person concerned what would make the difference.
3. Choose to demonstrate a positive attitude towards two people this week, without having anything in particular to tell or ask them. (Smiles, friendly greetings, interest in them as individuals all do this – it's very simple.)

CHAPTER 7

USING FEEDBACK

KEY LEARNING POINTS

- ■ noticing reactions
- ■ asking for feedback
- ■ receiving feedback
- ■ giving feedback
- ■ using feedback constructively

NOTES TO MANAGER/COACH

Be aware that you will be giving and receiving feedback during this session. As that is the topic under discussion, your group members will be particularly aware of the example you are setting, so ensure that your use of feedback is constructive.

With Exercise 30, you may want to ask people to prepare beforehand to save time during the session. You may also choose to go first, to set the example. Make sure it doesn't turn into grand presentation mode – keep it simple and informal.

INTRODUCTION

In the last chapter, we looked at how to convey your message effectively, and, as part of that, I suggested that it was important to notice people's response. In this chapter, we will explore the usefulness of finding out more about their response, to increase your ability to handle people well. We will also look at the way in which you give others information about your response to them, to ensure that you do this in a way that enhances the relationship.

WHAT IS FEEDBACK?

The word 'feedback' first came into use with the advent of computer technology and systems theory. It was a way of describing the loop of action and reaction (Figure 7.1).

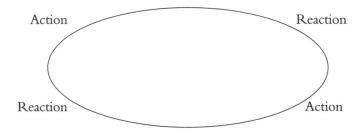

FIGURE 7.1   The feedback loop – every action produces a reaction

What was important about the identification of this feedback loop was the realization that every action produces a reaction and every reaction produces an action, and that it is hard to separate out cause from effect. Because it is a loop, it is difficult to identify where something starts – everything affects everything else.

I'm stating this because we have tended to lose this important realization as we've brought feedback into common use. We don't see it as part of a process, but rather as an end-point. If we are to use feedback well, we need to reassert that it is part of the process of relating to others, giving us information about their reaction that will affect our actions and reactions with them.

NOTICING REACTIONS

The most common feedback we receive is that which is given unconsciously. It is the immediate response or reaction to what we have done or said. This is not specific feedback – it doesn't usually give detail – it is simply on some scale of 1–10, with 1 being negative and 10 being positive.

Its usefulness is that it tells us if we are going in the right direction or not, but it doesn't tell us how to find the right direction if we're not. This would not be a problem most of the time if we took more notice of the small signs that say we're losing it. But most of us wait until there is a big negative sign before we take any notice!

Scenario – Noticing the response

Mike wanted his assistant to give a presentation to the team meeting the following week. He went to find Jane to talk to her about it. She was at her computer, obviously concentrating on what she was doing. Mike sat down beside her and said: 'Jane, I want to talk to you about the team meeting next week.' She was unresponsive, and carried on with what she was doing, although she had lost some of her concentration.

'Will you give a presentation on the Health and Safety Conference we went to last week?' Mike asked. 'Yes, of course,' snapped Jane.

'Can we talk about what points you will raise?' said Mike. Jane stopped what she was doing and turned to him angrily. 'Do you doubt my ability to prepare this properly? Why don't you do it yourself if you don't think I'll say the right thing? After all, you were there, too, and you seem to have time on your hands!'

If Mike had taken notice of the early signs that this was not the right moment to discuss the presentation, he would have avoided this outburst, and both of them would have felt better about the situation.

Most of us are aware when our communication is not

having the effect we want, but rather than stop and try a different tack, we carry on, in the vain hope that it will still work out all right. We need to learn to take notice of the early warning signals, so that we don't create bigger obstacles for ourselves to overcome.

In Chapter 4, I described in detail how to give attention to others. Just a few seconds of attention will quickly give you information about their response, and enable you to change tack.

ASKING FOR FEEDBACK

When you're not sure what someone's reaction is, asking them can be very useful. However, we need to guide the feedback they give, as most people are not good at giving useful information about their reactions. When people stop to think about their reaction, they will usually rationalize it, and try to justify it. This is often not helpful, because it doesn't tell us what we can do to elicit a more useful response.

Typically we will ask, 'What do you think?' and the response is likely to be: 'Quite interesting', or 'Sounds fine to me'. This doesn't tell us about their real reaction, and certainly doesn't help us to improve our way of conveying a message.

If we persist in asking what their reaction was, people are likely to find a negative response, because they think that is what we are asking for: 'I liked it, but I don't think it will work.'

So we need to ask the right questions to elicit the sort of information we want. Examples of useful questions about feedback would be:

- What do you think I was trying to convey to you?
- What worked for you in what I said?
- What worked for you in what I did?
- What would you have liked me to do differently?
- How would you have preferred me to behave?
- How would you have preferred me to give you the information?

- What do you now intend to do as a result of our conversation?
- What did you find useful in our conversation?

Exercise 29 – Asking for feedback

Work in pairs. Each one in turn is to tell the other about something you enjoy doing. At the end, ask the other person for feedback, using some of the questions listed above.

Talk in the whole group about what you discovered about feedback.

I am not suggesting that you should do this with every conversation you have with others, but you can do it with conversations where it is important to check that you have conveyed your message accurately. Remember that we all view the world differently, and that it is easy to misinterpret someone's intention or message.

I would rather someone had another go at getting their message across to me, by using a slightly different approach, than go away with a wrong interpretation.

USING FEEDBACK YOU'VE ASKED FOR

One use of feedback is to give me the chance to have another go, if my original version didn't convey the message I wanted.

Another use is to help you gradually to improve your way of interacting with others. You will notice that the questions cover both what I say and what I do.

When I notice a positive reaction, I will often ask, 'What did I do/say that worked for you?' I want to know how I elicited that positive reaction, so that I can use it again.

Most people are not immediately aware of what caused them to react, but when you ask the question you will usually get a response. They may start with, 'I don't know ...', but wait, and you will get something like, 'but when you mentioned x it switched me on', or 'but when you sat down beside me, I felt more comfortable'.

In finding out what works with others, you can gather a

repertoire of ways of conveying your message effectively. By using these, you reduce the number of times you fail to elicit the response you want.

You can use a similar learning approach to feedback when it is not positive. You will notice that the questions ask what would have been a preferred approach. It's not useful to find out what was wrong without finding out also what would have made it better. By knowing what would have been preferable, you have information on how to improve your communication in a way that would work for the other person. Otherwise, you just have to guess at what else to do or say.

RECEIVING FEEDBACK

Sometimes you don't need to ask for feedback – it is given to you anyway. Our attitude to feedback affects how much we receive, and what form it comes in. It is important, therefore, to receive feedback in a constructive way.

RECEIVING POSITIVE FEEDBACK

It is surprising, considering how much most of us like to feel valued and recognized, that we are generally so poor at receiving positive feedback.

Someone says to us that they liked the way we put something over to them, or that they appreciated the way we respected their need to finish the task in hand before embarking on our own conversation. Our response to such comments is usually dismissive – we find it embarrassing. Rather than say thank you, we will say, 'Oh, I'm not sure it was that good', or 'It was nothing'.

So the person doesn't bother to comment the next time, and we end up feeling that they *don't* value us!

By appreciating and acknowledging positive feedback, we encourage people to give us more, and we need it to help us to stay aware of what's working in our interactions with others, as well as to help us to feel good!

RECEIVING NEGATIVE FEEDBACK

Unfortunately, it is far more common to receive unasked for negative feedback in our culture. We seem to always tend towards noticing what's wrong rather than noticing what's right. If someone says to me, 'Can I give you some feedback?', I think to myself automatically, 'Uh, oh, what did I do wrong?', and I'm usually right – they will usually be critical.

However, we have a choice about how we react to the criticism. We can be defensive, or feel offended, or we can take it as an opportunity to learn what would have worked better, from this person's perspective.

Usually they will start by saying what was wrong, or what they didn't like. Most people stop at that point, but if you want to learn from their feedback, you need to prompt them on to the next stage.

You accept their statement and then ask, 'So, what would have worked better for you?' This way, you find out what would improve the interaction from their perspective, and have more strategies to use, with them and with others, in the future.

Scenario – Asking for feedback

Mike felt guilty and frustrated after the interaction with Jane about her presentation. He had a feeling that he had caused her to be so angry, and he didn't like to think that she really thought so badly of him.

After some consideration, he decided to confront the situation with Jane. He went back to her desk, where she was staring at her computer, angry and upset, and no longer able to concentrate anyway.

He apologized for interrupting again, and asked if she could spare ten minutes sometime during the next two hours. She said that it might as well be now, so they went to his office.

Mike started by saying that he wanted to clear up what had happened. He felt bad about the situation and wanted to rectify it if possible. He asked Jane to tell him what he had done to upset her.

Jane said he seemed to not care about what anyone else was doing, or how busy they were. If he wanted something, he just assumed that it was more important than anything else. She also said that she hadn't meant to be insulting to him, but she was angry at being interrupted and it had slipped out.

Rather than defend his position, Mike said he was sorry that he gave her that impression, and asked her: 'What should I have done differently?'

Jane said: 'If you had noticed that I was concentrating on what I was doing, and had asked when we could speak, the whole thing would have been different. Or even if you had left it at that moment, and come back a little bit later, when I had finished what I was doing.'

Mike thanked her, and then asked, 'So when could we talk about the presentation?' Jane laughed, and said, 'Can we do it in about an hour when I've pulled myself together, and finished that damn job on the computer?'

Mike agreed and thanked her for helping him to rectify the situation. 'No, thank **you**,' she said. 'Most people wouldn't bother, and I feel better about it now. I'm just sorry I was so rude to you.'

The net result of discussions like this is to benefit both sides. The relationship is improved, rather than just returned to where it was before. We all have increased respect for someone who uses negative feedback well, and takes notice of what we have to say. And the person receiving the feedback can learn how to improve their way of relating.

GIVING FEEDBACK

The other side of the loop is giving feedback to others about how their way of relating or communicating with you affects you. We all do this automatically through our behaviour, our attitude or our response, but, as I have already commented, people frequently ignore this feedback and do not take it into account. By consciously giving them information, you ensure that they are aware of your reaction. This will help them to improve their people skills as well, should they choose to use the information.

It is vital to be aware of the tendency we all have only to offer feedback about what's wrong. I have already discussed this in the previous section. When giving feedback, remember that your intention is to elicit a positive reaction from the other person, and to help them to deal with you more effectively.

GIVING POSITIVE FEEDBACK

Do bother to tell people what they did that worked well for you! It makes them feel good, and it increases the likelihood of them using a similar tack in the future.

Make sure that you give them specific information:

- 'It made such a difference when you reminded me that we had already done most of the work for this project while working on the one two weeks ago.'
- 'I felt much more comfortable when you suggested that we discussed this over a cup of coffee.'
- 'I liked the way you presented the info as a flow chart.'

Many discussions of feedback conclude that you should give positive feedback first, before any negative comments. This often leads to people finding some vaguely positive thing to say, which they rush out before getting to the meat of the matter – their criticisms. This frequently feels like what it is – a throw-away line to pay lip-service to good practice.

It does matter that you make a conscious effort to find some positive feedback to offer someone, and that it is genuine. There is always something that worked – at a minimum, the fact that they approached you in the first place. And do make sure that you say it with feeling, so that the person concerned knows you mean it.

Notice that often the problem with giving positive feedback is not finding something to say, it's bothering to say it, particularly if you have nothing negative to add! I am still surprised by how many people will praise someone else to other people, but not to the person concerned!

Finally, remember that positive feedback is merely reinforcement of something that worked – it doesn't have to be fulsome praise. In fact, inappropriate praise can feel almost insulting: 'I thought that cup of tea you made was the best I've ever tasted – well done!' is inappropriate. 'Thank you for the tea – it just touched the spot!' is more useful. Someone praising highly a fairly ordinary gesture or statement can make you wonder if they think you are stupid. Simple thank yous and expressions of appreciation or recognition are more acceptable, and feel more genuine.

GIVING NEGATIVE FEEDBACK

I would suggest that there is a simple rule for this: Don't!

On its own, negative feedback does nothing useful. It reinforces your negativity as you give it, and it produces a defensive or hurt reaction in the other person. We cannot help but feel put down when we receive negative feedback, and it is hard, when we feel like that, to think positively about what we can do about it.

Scenario – The effect of negative feedback

I remember vividly an incident at school that inhibited my writing skills for years. I had submitted my first proper essay for English, and was quite proud of it, having worked on it for several hours.

When I received it back, the teacher had written on it: 'Too pedantic' and given me a C. I was upset, but determined to do better next time. I looked up pedantic in the dictionary and found it meant long-winded.

My next essay was only one and a half pages long. I had carefully edited it to make just the main points. When

I received it back, she had written, 'Not long enough' on it and given me a C again. I went up to her and asked her what I should do to get it right. She said I should aim for something between the two!

I lost my enthusiasm for English and chose not to do English at A level as a result of her lack of care in giving feedback.

GIVING CONSTRUCTIVE FEEDBACK

I am not suggesting that you don't ever tell people what they did wrong. It's a major part of our learning for all of us, to make mistakes and learn to rectify them. And whereas mistakes in analysis, logic or mechanics tend to be obvious, it is far more difficult to know when you have made a mistake in an interaction with someone. There are so many factors that may affect their reactions, and often the response is cloaked, and we don't notice the adverse reaction until much later.

Many times it isn't that you have made an obvious mistake in your interaction with someone. It's just that you could have handled it more effectively, and saved yourself and them effort.

I therefore recommend that the feedback you give is based on what would have been even better than what they did:

'I would have liked it better if you had ... '
'I would have been more comfortable if you had ... '
'I would have responded more positively if you had ... '

It is also important to make your statements as specific as possible. Tell them exactly what they should have said or done, rather than saying it should have been different.

EXAMPLES

- 'I would have liked it better if you had given me a written outline to follow and make notes on.'
- 'I would have been more comfortable if you had suggested

we met somewhere less formal than your office, such as the coffee area.'
- 'I would have responded more positively if you had made it obvious how this was relevant to my work at the start.'

Exercise 30 – Giving constructive feedback

Each member of the group is to tell the rest of the group about something they have been doing recently.

Take ten minutes to prepare what you want to say. Keep it brief and informal.

Now ask each person in turn to offer their information. At the end, the rest of the group gives feedback. This can be positive, or constructive, or a mixture of both. The group monitors each other's feedback to ensure that it meets the criteria listed above.

Afterwards you may choose to discuss what you have realized about feedback.

'NEUTRAL' FEEDBACK

It is worth pointing out that there is another category of feedback that I call neutral. This is where we give a non-committal response when someone asks us, for example: 'How do you think that went?' 'It was all right', or 'It wasn't too bad'.

These types of neutral comments *always* imply that it could have been better. They don't come across as neutral, they come across as negative, because of the implication behind them. They are therefore not useful as feedback and should be avoided.

NON-VERBAL FEEDBACK

I have spent a lot of time discussing the verbal feedback we may give. It is important to remember that the majority of the feedback we give is non-verbal. It is the expression on our face, our obvious reactions, that normally give feedback.

We tend not to say: 'I wish you had waited until I'd finished what I was doing before launching into your subject.' Instead we frown, don't look at the person, try to continue with our task, and snap at them when we respond. And they sometimes 'get the message'. However, sometimes they don't, so clarify your feedback verbally, so that they can't ignore it. Preferably, do this as soon as it starts to go wrong, rather than waiting until you are really angry or upset. It is far easier to change what is going wrong at the beginning of the wrong direction rather than when it has already had a major negative impact. It is also kinder, both to yourself and to the other person.

Be aware of the non-verbal feedback you are giving. If it is positive, confirm the positive verbally. If it is negative, actively suggest what would improve the situation. And, of course, if it is not what you intend, change it!

CONCLUSION

We never stop giving and receiving feedback, in one form or another. Since it is such a constant, it is worth making sure that it is useful and constructive.

It is so easy to misinterpret someone's reaction when we are working with them, and for those misinterpretations to grow into causes of major conflict. It makes so much more sense to use feedback to learn, and to improve our relationships, by becoming active in asking for and giving constructive feedback.

ACTION LIST – USING FEEDBACK

1. Agree to give each other constructive feedback at least three times in the next week.
2. Notice when someone is not reacting positively and stop and ask them what would make it work better for them, or at least try something different.
3. Agree a team policy for giving feedback on presentations you give to the team.
4. After an interaction with someone outside this group, ask the person concerned for feedback.
5. Practise giving positive feedback, unasked for, to four people this week.

PART 2

APPLYING PEOPLE SKILLS

PART 2

In this part, we will explore various applications of the skills we have been discussing. This will give you a chance to reinforce the specific skills and check out how they integrate together to improve your overall people skills in specific work situations.

I have chosen to look at the areas where people are most likely to find it difficult to maintain their good practice, as these are the places where we most need to use the skills!

CHAPTER 8

USING PEOPLE SKILLS IN FORMAL MEETINGS

KEY LEARNING POINTS

- clarify intentions and outcomes
- getting ready for meetings
- paying attention in meetings
- dealing with red herrings
- respecting others' views
- putting your point across
- involving everyone

NOTES TO MANAGER/COACH

There are several references to previous sessions in this chapter. If people can't remember, they should be encouraged to go back and have another look at them.

Remind yourself of what you covered in those sessions, so you can prompt them.

INTRODUCTION

It is easy, in meetings, to slip into 'meeting' mode, isn't it! There are very few situations where someone will say, 'Oh good, I've got another meeting now'. It's more likely to be, 'Here we go, another damn meeting!' And with the statement go a whole set of ready-made reactions – physical posture, facial expression, mindset – that are put on like a uniform.

Scenario – A typical team meeting

The weekly team meeting has just got under way. As the team leader looks round the table, she realizes that she is seeing a familiar scene, which is unlikely to lead to a very positive meeting.

James is sitting opposite her, armed with a sheaf of papers, ready to do battle on whatever is on the agenda. Sue and Pete are sat either side of her, ready to show how loyal to her they are. In Pete's case it's quite genuine, but Sue is primarily after promotion. It shows in the way they respond as she catches their eyes: Pete smiles, relaxed and comforting; Sue is too eager to show interest.

Mark and Sam are in their usual positions, looking bored already, and the meeting hasn't started yet. And Phillipa is busy writing something that will have nothing to do with this agenda – she hates wasting time, and resents having to come to meetings.

Bob is already trying to look inconspicuous. He dreads being asked for his opinion, or asked to report at meetings, and always hopes that the dominant ones will fill the time.

Do you recognize any of these characters? I have seen variations on this thousands of times in a whole variety of meetings! Sometimes one type is prevalent – they all look bored – but there is usually a mixture in any group. Why do we react like this to meetings?

THE REASON FOR MEETINGS

There is much written about how to improve meetings, but we are going to concentrate on the use of people skills to improve them.

The problem is that most people regard meetings as an information-giving exercise. They are not seen as an opportunity for people to relate to and work with each other.

This is a strange distortion. When we meet with friends, we don't think of it as being primarily information-giving. It is a chance to talk, catch up and enjoy each other's company. If you just want to pass on some information, you will tend to write it and pass it or send it to them.

CLARIFYING THE INTENTION OF MEETINGS

The first step to improving meetings is to clarify the overall intention of the meeting. If you are the person organizing it, you can do this yourself; if you are one of those attending, you can ask the organizer, to prompt them into thinking it through.

The original intention of most meetings is to utilize the interaction of a variety of people to enrich the results or conclusions. It is therefore a question of bringing this to the fore, rather than changing the intention.

Just as we considered clarifying your intention when engaging one-to-one with someone (see Chapter 6), we need to think through the intention with a larger group meeting.

You can begin by considering the subject matter of the meeting.

- If it is purely information to be handed over, could you do it in a more effective way?
- If you want information to be used, how do you want it used?
- Do you want discussion, to air different viewpoints, and do you want that to lead to application of the information?
- Do you want some differing opinions on something, to help to reach a considered decision?

- Do you want specific input from individual areas of expertise?
- Do you want to use the information to promote discussion and interest among the meeting participants?

Obviously, in most formal meetings, there is an agenda of different items, and they may have slightly different intentions. However, the mere act of thinking of what you are using the information for will of itself liven up the agenda.

Then you can think about what you want as a result of the meeting, in its fullest sense. (See Chapter 6 on outcomes.)

1. *What immediate results do you want from the meeting?* This may be actions, agreement, a revised plan, commitment to a policy, or increased motivation, interest, and so on.
2. *What immediate effect do you want the meeting to have?* This may be people talking together, people feeling motivated, everyone enjoying the discussion, everyone joining in, lots of good ideas, people listening to each other, and so on.
3. *What longer-term effect do you want the meeting to have?* This may be evidence that agreed actions have been taken, everyone wanting to attend team meetings in the future, improved understanding between the participants in their everyday work, and so on.

WHY SHOULD ANYONE COME TO THE MEETING?
If you do this form of thinking through, you will have already realized that the meeting could be very worth while for participants. Now they need to realize this. The important question is: what makes it worth while for these people to attend it?

You can now express your intentions and outcomes for this meeting in a way which will appeal to the participants. Remember that they are all different, and different ways will be needed to attract them. (See Chapter 5.)

Exercise 31 – Planning the agenda of a meeting

Take your team meetings as an example, and plan how they could be made attractive. Do this in two small groups, so that you can compare and discuss your results.

1. Think about the overall intention of the meeting, and write that down.
2. Now list a typical agenda and note against each agenda item what the intention is with this.
3. Think through the results wanted, in the three categories, and write a short paragraph to express this in a way that will appeal to everyone.

Compare and discuss your results.

Example

1. This team meeting is intended to give people the opportunity to discuss the information from head office and to work out how we, as a team, can utilize it. It is also an opportunity to get to know each other and our individual work better.
2. Agenda
   (a) Report on overall productivity: discuss what we could do to improve this.
   (b) Report on Martin's project: find out what he's been doing and see how the rest of us can contribute.
   (c) Problems with equipment: identify what they are and what we can do about them.
   (d) Review our mission: discuss how we're doing and what the next steps are.
   (e) Name a success: something each of us has done that we're proud of.
   (f) A mistake to learn from: three 'mistakes' to be volunteered and what could be learnt from them.
   (g) Other information: a chance to ask questions of clarification about other information sent out with this agenda.
3. I want some more action steps on our overall mission, and equipment problems resolved. I want everyone to feel that the meeting is useful to them, and that they are more aware of what others in the team are doing, or trying to do. And please suggest agenda items for the next meeting that would interest you.

PREPARING YOURSELF FOR MEETINGS

Not only do you need to prepare for meetings by thinking through their intention, you also need to set yourself up for them, by thinking about your own attitude towards them.

The typical mindsets for meetings set you up to expect them to be boring or confrontational, and, of course, this means that you demonstrate the behaviour of someone who has that expectation. (See Chapter 2.)

It makes a significant difference to what happens in the meeting if you spend a few moments beforehand preparing yourself. Start by remembering some good meetings you have had. Remember how you were in them, physically and mentally, and begin to set yourself up to be like that for this one.

We often think that we can't change it, if the meeting is run by someone else, or if the majority seem content to leave it as it is. However, **any** individual in a meeting can make some difference to what happens, by setting a different example to others through how they behave.

Scenario – Changing the tone of the meeting

Mark decided that he was fed up being bored by his meetings. He spent a lot of time going to them, and he didn't want to feel that it was time wasted.

He decided to see if he could make some difference to what happened. He remembered a meeting he had really enjoyed. It was with people he hadn't met before and they were all asked to say something about their work at the beginning, so everyone spoke. He remembered how his interest had been caught, and how, after speaking at the beginning, he had joined in more for the rest of the meeting.

He decided to act as if he were at a similar meeting. He would walk in and sit by someone he didn't know very well, rather than take his usual place next to Sam. He would talk to this person in the break, and find out about what they did. And he would suggest that the first item on the agenda was everyone saying a few words about something they were presently engaged in. He spoke to his manager and asked her if they could add his suggestion to the beginning of the agenda.

She was surprised by the change in his demeanour, but agreed to his proposal. He sat next to Sue, and chatted to her before the meeting started. She had always ignored him, but when he asked her about the results of her project, she became quite animated, and forgot her usual role of trying to impress the manager. He had already made a difference.

Exercise 32 – Improving the quality of team meetings

1. Think about your team meetings again. Individually, think of one way in which you could contribute to improving the quality of your team meetings. Share the ideas in the whole group, giving recognition to every individual's idea.
2. Now think about a different formal meeting which you attend, and identify one way you could make a difference in that meeting. Help each other to find ideas by talking about them in small groups of two or three.

By making the decision to behave differently in meetings, and to approach them with different expectations, we can all contribute to making them more effective.

THE FEAR OF FORMAL MEETINGS

There is one category of our behaviour in meetings that needs particular attention. It is when we are anxious or awed by the meeting. This is likely to be the case if it is not a type of meeting we are familiar with, for example, if you are called into a senior management meeting, to give a presentation on a particular topic, or if it is time for the annual appraisals.

Your state of anxiety will affect significantly the way in which you present yourself at that meeting. It is therefore particularly important to take control of your state beforehand. Go through all the steps in Chapter 2, and make sure that you are at your best before you go in.

It is also useful to remember that the other people in the room are not ogres! They will probably all have experienced a similar fear to yours at some point in their lives, and will be sympathetic, if you expect them to be. They want you to do your best, and are not usually deliberately intending to trip you up. For them, this is another normal meeting, and you just happen to be joining in this time. Imagine that they are a familiar group for you, and smile at people. You'll be surprised at how easy it is to elicit friendly looks!

So far, we've looked at the preparation for meetings. You may notice that I've said nothing about preparing information. That's obviously important, but you know that! You may be less aware of how important the people dynamic is to the success of a meeting. Clarifying the intention and outcomes, and setting yourself up ready for the meeting make a significant difference, and they only take a few moments.

USING PEOPLE SKILLS DURING MEETINGS

All the points I've made so far about how we relate to others effectively apply to meetings. Again, each one of us can take responsibility for treating others respectfully, regardless of whether we are leading the meeting or not.

LISTENING TO OTHERS

If you look around for a moment during a meeting, while someone is speaking, you will usually be able to spot two dominant behaviours:

1. *'Switching off'* Because they are not the centre of attention, and because they are not interested in the subject, people let their minds wander.

2. *'Waiting to go'* These people are not listening to what's being said, they are waiting to be able to have their say. It may be on the same topic, but it is unlikely to be related to what's being said now, because they are not listening!

We were given two ears and one mouth. They should be used proportionally! In fact, if everyone paid attention to whoever was speaking during meetings, there would be a significant improvement in the process:

- We would each feel valued when speaking.
- We would find out more about each other if we switched on full attention (see Chapter 4).
- We would keep the conversation relevant, by referring to each other's points.
- We would not repeat unnecessarily – have you noticed how often people make the same point or ask the same question because they weren't listening?

RECOGNIZING RED HERRINGS

Many meetings are sabotaged by someone going off at a tangent from the subject in hand, and then others joining in. These red herrings can slow down the process of a meeting, and increase the frustration of those who find meetings a waste of time anyway.

If we pay full attention, and have clarified the purpose of agenda items, these irrelevancies can be controlled.

Scenario – Red herrings

The team meeting was under way, and had reached item three on the agenda: Problems with equipment. The group have identified the problem of incompatible soft-ware, and are looking at possible solutions.

Pete   Since most of us are using the same spreadsheet package now, it would make sense for James and Sue to start using it as well, then we'll be compatible on that one.

James	That is a lousy package. Mine has far more sophistication, and I think everyone should update to match it.
Pete	What do you use it for, James?
James	That's not the point. I prefer to be up to date.
Mark	What does it matter, James? It's not that important.
Sue	**How is this discussion helping us to resolve the problem?**

By paying attention, Sue is able to identify the start of a red herring, and question if it is relevant. Without her question, there could well have been a lengthy argument about relative merits of a particular piece of software – interesting to some, but not useful in this meeting.

Exercise 33 – Dealing with red herrings

Think of several 'red herrings' you have experienced recently in meetings. In pairs, state briefly the red herring and decide how you could have pointed out its irrelevancy, respectfully. Share your ideas with the whole group. (You may choose to agree on a challenge to be used in your team meetings when anyone thinks the discussion is becoming irrelevant.)

It is important to remember that sometimes an apparent red herring is valuable.

- It may lead to an awareness that more information is needed before you make a decision.
- It may demonstrate that there is another issue which you also need to consider.
- It may highlight that someone feels very strongly about something – useful information when dealing with that person.
- It may involve members of the meeting in discussion who don't usually join in.

It is up to the leader of the meeting to give recognition to and weigh up the value of the red herring within the context of the overall intention of the meeting.

PUTTING YOUR POINT ACROSS

Obviously, in meetings, you will be expected to express opinions, join in discussions and suggest ideas. If you have bothered to listen carefully, you can do this far more effectively.

We have already looked at ways of presenting your message clearly (Chapter 6), and these apply to meetings as to any other form of interaction.

You also need to remember to recognize and work with the differences in the group. (See Chapter 5 for more on this.) By gearing what you say to meet the requirements of different people within the group, you increase the likelihood of your ideas being accepted. In particular, it is important during discussions to avoid dismissing the points made by the person speaking before you. By doing so, you lose their support, and that of anyone agreeing with them.

One favourite way of being dismissive is by saying, 'Yes, *but* . . .'. Every time someone says this, you know that they don't agree with you! What this provokes in most of us is a desire to argue our case more strongly, by responding with a 'yes, but . . .' of our own.

We need to find a more useful way of expressing a different point of view that doesn't dismiss the other person's opinion or idea. The first change that needs to be made is to change that word 'but'. If you simply change 'but' to 'and', you already change the tone of what's being said. 'But' dismisses what went before. 'And' adds another dimension.

You can improve on this change further by acknowledging what the person said in your response.

Examples

- I can understand why x matters to you. I also think we need to consider y.
- I like your point about x and it leads me to think y might also help.

■ I, too, want to see x happen, and I wonder if we could
   look at it from a different perspective as well.

Exercise 34 – People skills in discussions

Form into two groups. Choose a contentious subject for
discussion, (either a work topic, or a 'social' topic like nuclear
energy).

  As you discuss, practise paying attention to each other, and
presenting your point of view in ways that respect others'
opinions. (And, of course, challenge irrelevancies if they occur.)

  Allow the discussion to run for 15 minutes, then discuss in
the whole group what happened.

INVOLVING EVERYONE

One of the reasons some people don't like meetings is because
they feel that they are obliged to make a contribution. There
can be intense pressure to say something when there is a
discussion, and this can make people very uncomfortable.
Sometimes the discomfort is because they really don't have
anything to add to the discussion. Sometimes it is because
they fear that the more forceful personalities in the meeting
will ride roughshod over any ideas they put forward.
Sometimes it's because the discussion goes on so quickly that
their ideas no longer fit the point in the discussion.

  Often the approach taken to overcome this is to pounce
on someone and say, 'Simon, what do you think?' I have
always felt that this is a rather cruel approach, and likely to
make the person even more uncomfortable – hardly good
people skills.

  So the question is, how do you involve everyone usefully
in discussions and sharing of ideas?

  First you need to recognize that not everyone will want
to contribute to every discussion. Remember the two ears and
one mouth statement. Some people actively participate by
listening carefully, and nodding when they agree.

  To deal with those who don't contribute, even though
their contribution could be useful, it is important to look at

ways of making them comfortable with contributing. By taking away their anxiety, you will gain a useful contribution, better expressed because they are no longer anxious.

There are a couple of simple techniques for doing this which work well.

SETTING A DIFFERENT TONE

By making the approach to a discussion or collecting ideas slightly less serious, you can often encourage involvement from people who are worried about what their peers will think of them. This can only be achieved by asking if anyone has any silly ideas, and then accepting all ideas put forward. I have often found that extremely useful ideas will be put forward under this category, because nothing is wrong, so there's no danger of your idea being pulled apart.

Another way is to ask people to pose a question or suggest something as if they were someone else, such as a customer, or a new starter, or Einstein! This gives freedom from the constraint of being personally judged by what you say.

You can also set the tone that says that every idea is considered a positive idea and is to be treated as such by everyone else, and enforce it. You can set the example by suggesting an outrageous idea, and asking for positive feedback. After that, no one else will feel stupid in making a contribution.

USING A DIFFERENT METHOD

The second technique for involving everyone is to reduce the amount of whole group discussion and increase the amount of small group work. Most people feel more comfortable contributing in a small group, and the results are then presented as an amalgam of the ideas from the group, so no one feels singled out.

Small group work need not take long. I often give 5–10 minutes for a small group activity and then call them back. It can also give a more useful response, as the 'red herrings' are often eliminated by this method. It is important to give a specific task, rather than just say, 'discuss this for 10 minutes'.

Examples of structured group activity

- Between you, think of three ways of making this work.
- Come up with two things that might stop us achieving this, and then two possible ways past each obstacle.
- What can we use this information for?
- How many ways can you think of to implement this?

These techniques are obviously most easily suggested by the leader of the meeting. However, any of the participants can also suggest changing the tone, or the method. We **all** have a responsibility for making meetings work.

Scenario – Involving everyone

Paul had noticed that, at their team meetings, three of the team hardly spoke at all. At first he had thought it was because they had nothing to say, but he knew that John was great at coming up with ideas on a one-to-one basis, so thought that they probably all had something to offer.

At the next meeting, when they were asked to comment on a proposal, he said that he had a really silly question to ask, which was: why were they doing it? Another of the silent ones, Betty, nodded in agreement. 'I wondered that,' she said, 'and I also wonder whose responsibility it would be.' Paul was pleased with his success at getting one of them involved, and wanted to have another go.

Later on the chairman asked for ideas on how to implement a strategy. Paul jumped in first. 'Could we do this on flip charts, in two groups, like we did at the away-day?'

The chairman agreed, and that method was used. Everyone contributed, and also joined in with the following whole group discussion.

REMEMBER, WE'RE ALL HUMAN

Throughout this session, we have been exploring simple ways of making meetings more effective by using our people skills. These are skills we use quite naturally in some situations, and then forget in situations where we feel under pressure or inhibited.

Even a formal meeting is composed of ordinary human beings, who have their likes and dislikes, strengths and weaknesses, and who are essentially just like us!

We all respond to a smile, a considerate gesture, an acknowledgement of our worth. We all enjoy a laugh sometimes, we all like to feel we're doing something useful.

If you do nothing else, remember that these people are all human, will not devour you, and will respond to recognition of their and your humanity.

Someone said to me that his biggest fear of presenting to his peers was that they could be sitting there going, 'Why him? I could do it better'. I suggested that he started by saying, 'It's terrifying presenting to you lot – so thank God that it's me not you doing it!' He thought about it for a moment, and said, 'You're right. They'll laugh at that, and then feel some sympathy for me'. It's a way of acknowledging our human-ness.

ACTION LIST – USING PEOPLE SKILLS IN FORMAL MEETINGS

1. Agree a definition for the intention and outcomes of your team meetings. Give everyone a copy and refer to it at each meeting and for compiling each agenda.
2. Before your next formal meeting, set yourself up ready for it to be constructive and useful.
3. Plan to practise paying attention and acknowledging others' viewpoints in two meetings coming up.
4. Agree a set of 'ground rules' for your team meetings about how you will all behave.

5. Practise saying, 'Yes, and ...' instead of 'Yes, but ...'. You may even agree in your team meeting ground rules that 'but' is a banned word.

6. If you notice that some aren't involved in discussions, or if you tend not to get involved, find a way to make involvement comfortable in the next meeting you attend.

CHAPTER 9

Working in a Team

KEY LEARNING POINTS

- **benefits of team working**
- **having a common vision**
- **agreeing team behaviours**
- **valuing and using differences**
- **valuing and using strengths**
- **maintaining relationships**
- **exchanging skills**

NOTES TO MANAGER/COACH

In Exercise 38, make sure that everyone is given credit for some strengths. It's important that everyone feels valued.

INTRODUCTION

Nowadays it is common practice to work in teams, and there is an assumption that this is a good thing to do. There is no doubt that multi-skilled and cross-functional teams will be the norm for most working practice in the future. They offer potentially the powerful combination of a variety of skills and perspectives being brought to bear on any task, so that everything is tackled more effectively and more imaginatively. However, for this potential to be the reality of how teams work together, there needs to be considerable work on bringing the team into a cohesive whole.

Historically, we have worked in a very individualistic way, competing with our peers to be best. It requires a radical change of mindset to move from individual competitiveness to team co-operation.

CHANGING THE MINDSET

To start with, we have to revise our beliefs about individualism. The easiest way to work on that is consciously to identify the benefits of working in a team. This is not the benefits as identified by the organization, but personal benefits, such as being able to call on the experience of other team members when tackling something you haven't done before.

Exercise 35 – Benefits of working in a team

As a group, list the potential benefits for individuals of working in a team. Collect as many different ones as you can.

By focusing your mind on the benefits that working in a team could bring to you personally, you do two things:

1. You make it more attractive for you and begin to counteract the benefits in individualism.
2. You start noticing how you might enable the potential benefits to become reality.

BRINGING THE TEAM TO A SHARED VISION

Teams are set up to achieve particular goals. They have a shared task. What is needed to make the team more cohesive is a shared vision, that is, how they will achieve the tasks, and how they will work together.

By setting an ideal vision of their work and how it is done, a group can develop a real sense of purpose, and a reason for overcoming difficulties they may have in working together.

Scenario – A team vision

We are a highly successful team. We are like the crew of a cruise ship, all working at our different roles to achieve success between us. Everyone plays an important part, and if anyone is having problems, anyone who can will help out. We are constantly aware of external conditions, and potential changes in them, and ready to change tack if need be. We keep each other's morale high, so that pressure doesn't get us down. We work with our customers, so that both they and we enjoy the process. We keep the records clearly and effectively so that we do not have problems there that slow us down in our main goal. We have fun at what we do.

By using a metaphor – like the crew of a cruise ship – you can develop the theme further, and identify the way you work together to achieve your goals.

Exercise 36 – A team vision and purpose

How would you describe your team's purpose and vision? Discuss in the whole group, and use metaphors to help. (You may decide to choose one that you all like as your team vision.)

TEAM BEHAVIOUR

Once you have a common vision for the team, you have already begun to identify some of the behaviours that will help you to achieve this vision. We cannot take for granted that people will behave co-operatively or constructively within a team. Remember that most of us have been taught to behave competitively, and we need to revise our behaviours to be effective in a team.

So the team need to agree some team behaviours, so that everyone knows that these are the norm, and anything that counteracts the agreement can be challenged.

EXAMPLES OF TEAM BEHAVIOURS
- We will respect each other's viewpoints.
- We will help each other out if need be.
- We will share information.
- We will support each other.
- We will present a coherent front to our customers.

Exercise 37 – Team behaviours

You have already looked at ground rules for team meetings (see Chapter 8). What would you add to that, or change, to have agreed team working behaviours in general? Divide into two groups and come up with lists, then compare and discuss.

The team behaviours are really just making overt how we can work co-operatively, so that everyone knows the 'rules'.

Once these team definitions are in place, the context is set for individuals to play their part in making the team an effective body. If you are in a team where these definitions don't exist, you may like to suggest that the team spends a little time creating them. If that doesn't seem possible to you, there are still ways in which you can apply your people skills to make a difference to the effectiveness of team working.

BUILDING RELATIONSHIPS

We have spent a lot of time looking at how we can build relationships to enhance the way we work with others. All the principles we have covered apply to working in teams.

FINDING OUT ABOUT DIFFERENCE

The team consists of a variety of individuals, who are all different, and all of whom have something valuable to contribute.

As one of these individuals, you can make the effort to find out about the others in the team. Informal chats at break-times, before or after team meetings, can give you a lot of valuable information.

It still surprises me how little people who work together know about each other. Hobbies, interests and preferences are all easy to find out about, and can help in enabling us to work more effectively with that person. You may have noticed that in many of the exercises you have been talking to each other in pairs or threes, and found out more about each other. This is likely to improve relationships, because it is positive in intent, and is first-hand information, not second-hand or impressionistic.

Scenario – Finding out about team members

Joseph and Rose have been put into the same customer service team. They came from different backgrounds: her from marketing, him from engineering. They had vaguely known each other by sight before. She thought he seemed dour and pedantic, he thought she was rather flighty.

During a team event, they were paired up, and asked to find out about each other and report back on the other person. They discovered they both loved music, and in fact both played musical instruments, albeit only for fun.

Joseph found that Rose was a meticulously organized person who hated mess, and liked things to be finished off properly. He also discovered that she understood the new procedures for customer service – very useful, as he didn't!

Rose found that Joseph also liked to be organized and to know exactly what he had to do. She also found him to be very friendly, once he got over his shyness.

The two people in the scenario could work together much more effectively once they knew a bit more about each other, and their story is not unusual. By finding out what others in the team are like, we can all make it easier to work with them. (For more on this, see Chapter 5.)

MAINTAINING RAPPORT

Part of what you're doing when you bother to find out about people is establishing rapport. This really means that you have built a foundation on a personal level for a working relationship. (See Chapter 3 for more on this.)

It is important to remember to maintain it by keeping a personal touch in what you do. Simple examples like saying hello when you first go into the office, or meet another member of the team in the day, can make a lot of difference.

We forget that establishing rapport is not a one-off activity. If we neglect to make the personal contact in a positive way, it is easily lost.

Scenario – Losing rapport

Ken was up to his ears in work. He was feeling under a lot of pressure on this particular morning, and didn't even notice Ann come into the coffee lounge, where he'd gone to make a quick drink. Ann wondered how she'd upset him.

Later that day, Ken went up to Ann to ask her about something. She was quite sharp with him, and he wondered what he'd done to upset her, but he hadn't time to worry about it.

An apparently trivial event like this can grow out of all proportion, and become a hostile relationship, because neither party stopped and bothered to re-establish rapport.

GIVING TIME TO THE RELATIONSHIPS

In a team it is easy to be totally task-driven, particularly in the sort of work atmospheres we tend to have today, where there is always more to do than time to do it in, and it has become the norm to work extra hours to try to fit it all in.

Yet in the longer term, we save time if we give some space to establishing good relationships with other members of the team. By showing an interest in others, we make it more likely that they will show an interest in us.

It only takes a moment to stop to make sure that you're not imposing an irritable mood from something else on to your contact with this person, and to make the contact positive. The pay-off is the gradual build-up of a level of rapport that allows you to forget occasionally!

BE INTERESTED IN THEIR WORK

Although you're in a team, it's easy to get totally involved in your own priorities, and regard them as being the only thing that really matters. Often, the reason that team members don't benefit from each other's experience is because they don't know what each other is doing, so can't offer or ask for relevant help.

A simple question, 'What are you working on?', can keep you up to date with others' work, and give you useful information about where your areas of work may overlap – where you have something useful to offer, or where they may be useful to you. Further, this expression of interest helps to make the person feel valued for what they are doing.

USING THE STRENGTHS OF THE TEAM

One of the main reasons for forming a team is to gain the benefit of the diverse strengths of the individuals involved. Yet this is rarely exploited fully.

The obvious strengths may be utilized – a sales person to sell, an administrator to administrate, etc. – but the individual strengths are rarely explored in more detail than this. Yet there are likely to be: good risk-takers; ones with a lively sense of humour; ones who are very organized; people who always finish things off; creative problem-solvers; ones who are good at graphics; good devil's advocates; and so on.

It is not just a mixture of technical skills that makes a good team, it is the mixture of personal qualities and characteristics and their effective use that will transform the team into an excellent one.

Scenario – Being valuable to the team

Tim was a member of a particular assembly team. It was clear to the new team leader that he didn't play his part in the assembly very effectively. Yet the rest of the team seemed to like him and protect him. His lack of efficiency didn't seem to bother them. The team leader was curious about this and started to ask questions.

He discovered that Tim always noticed how others were and showed concern if they were a bit down or fed up. He also had a great sense of humour and kept the team morale high. Because he had worked on this assembly for a long time, he knew what to do if anything went wrong, and the others called on him to advise them if they weren't sure. He also took newcomers under his wing and showed them the best way of doing the job.

Tim was invaluable to the team, and they were only too happy to make up for the fact that he no longer did the actual job effectively. The team leader realized that what Tim did for the team was worth far more than what he was supposed to do, and he suggested that they make him 'trouble-shooter' to the team, and take over his part in the line. The team and Tim were delighted to be able to have him openly take the role he had already been playing unofficially.

Exercise 38 – The strengths of the team

What are the strengths of your team? List on a flip chart some of the personal characteristics that each person could contribute to the team. Concentrate on the non-technical abilities.

Discuss how you could use these strengths more effectively to improve the team achievements.

EXCHANGE OF SKILLS

If team strengths are to be used well, it's important that there is some exchange agreed, a balance of use. I remember discovering that someone was excellent at laying out documents. 'Don't tell the others,' he said, 'or I'll get landed with all the reports to do, and I'll never get my own work done.' This could have been a real asset to the team, but first the others would need to decide how they could help him out with his own work.

You often find this bartering happens in a family situation. The child asks for help with their homework, and dad agrees, if the child will help him do the washing-up afterwards. This maintains the balance, so no one's individual responsibilities are being neglected. It also makes everyone feel better. No one is being exploited and no one is under any obligation because they have asked a favour.

In a team, it may not always work on a direct exchange basis – I'll do this for you, if you'll do that for me – but it's important to remember the need for exchange.

Scenario – Exchanging skills

Robin didn't mind word-processing the odd document for Jenny. He knew she was slow at it, and he found it easy. She was relieved when he volunteered to help out and wondered what she could do in return.

Bob suggested that she could use the spare time to help him with planning his presentations. He always found it hard to think what to say, and she was good at it. Jenny pointed out that that didn't help Robin. Robin said that what he needed was someone to man the phone occasionally – he had constant interruptions from it.

Jenny said she would do half an hour on the phones whenever he did a document for her, and Bob said he'd do an hour a week as well, so everyone gained.

Exercise 39 – Exchanging skills

Have a short barter session, where you offer to use your strengths to help others, and collect or ask for specific offers in return. Make sure there's some form of balance in the exchanges.

USING DIFFERENT PERSPECTIVES

If you establish good working relationships in a team, then you can really benefit from the fact that all the members of the team have different perspectives. Once there is the 'safety zone' of what you have in common – the team vision and way of working, and the personal relationships that demonstrate that each person is valued for their strengths – then you can use the different perspectives to bring innovation and a broadening to your work.

What you have in a team is the potential of having an outsider's viewpoint with an insider's sympathy.

Scenario – Using a different perspective

Malcolm had to prepare for a meeting with a customer. He did his initial preparation, and asked Mary and Des if they could spare him half an hour to comment on it. They both agreed to meet with him that afternoon. Mary was very effective in dealing with customers, and he thought she could offer him some useful tips. Des used to work in this particular customer's type of industry, and could identify with what would matter to people in that industry.

They both helped him out in the way he wanted, and Mary also pointed out a couple of spelling mistakes – a useful addition!

To gain this sort of benefit from the diversity of the team, you need to ensure that everyone in the team is skilled at giving and receiving feedback. You need to know what sort of feedback you want, and ask the right questions. You also need to have the mindset that uses the feedback to improve things. On the other side of the loop, it is important to make sure that the feedback you give is constructive, and that you remember to give positive feedback as well! (See Chapter 7 for more on this.)

A WORKING RELATIONSHIP

There is some underlying assumption in team working that it is a prerequisite for an effective team that you like each other. Liking each other may be a by-product of developing the way you work with each other, but it's not a necessity for an effective team. We all tend to develop some personal friendships from work relationships, but it is unusual to find a whole team who are also personal friends.

What you need to establish is a basis for a working relationship, where you can respect each other, and benefit from working together. You may not like someone's personality, but you can find something to respect about what they do, and how they can contribute to the team. We don't have to accept the whole package, we have to look actively for a part of the package we can appreciate and find useful.

By setting up a shared vision and shared working practice that all agree to in the team, we have a set of criteria to use to find value in other members.

Scenario – Finding value in team members

A team I was a member of had become divided into two camps – the outgoing ones and the earnest ones. Our manager – one of the earnest ones – decided that she had to do something about it, as it was affecting the performance of the team. She called a meeting to discuss the problem.

Pat started it off. 'I don't like the way David and Di sit and laugh in the office.'

'What **do** you like about what they do?' asked our manager. Pat couldn't think of anything immediately. Our manager said, 'We've all agreed that we want to make our centre a friendly and welcoming place, and that we want to make our customers feel that they are receiving good value for money. How do they contribute to that vision?'

Pat then said that she knew the customers liked our work, and that David was the one in the team who went out of his way to greet customers, and make sure that they were comfortable.

'So what does Pat contribute?' asked our manager. We all began to shift our focus, and realize that we all had something to value and be valued for.

By the end of the session, we weren't friends, but we were more appreciative of each other's strengths, and we had realized that we needed both types of personalities for our centre to really thrive.

CONCLUSION

It is not easy to work together in a team in a really effective way. It takes some effort to bring a team together and to use the differences constructively, especially when it is not traditionally how people have worked.

The pay-offs for that effort make it worth while, and the application of our people skills within our own team is a priority. With the strength of an effective team behind us, our work improves and our relationship with others outside the team is easier to deal with.

ACTION LIST – WORKING IN A TEAM

1. Confirm a team vision within your team.
2. Agree your team behaviours.
3. Find out more about the strengths of two other people in your team this week.
4. Show an interest in the work of one other member of your team this week.
5. Agree to make some exchanges of skills with one or two other people.

CHAPTER 10

USING PEOPLE SKILLS IN DEALING WITH CONFLICT

KEY LEARNING POINTS

- ways of preventing conflict from developing
- learning to step back from conflicts and assess the situation
- finding common ground
- identifying the reason for the conflict
- changing the language of conflict

NOTES TO MANAGER/COACH

This is quite an emotional subject, and just discussing it may raise negative feelings in the team. Be ready to deal constructively with this if it happens, and look for ways of bringing some humour in to lighten the mood. Examples of domestic conflict normally make people laugh, especially if they are exaggerated.

INTRODUCTION

So far, we have explored the use of people skills in the context of normal interactions. The intention has been to find ways of improving working relationships, so that they become a strong foundation for effective working practice.

What we have not dealt with are the situations where our people skills tend to go completely out of the window, because of clashes of interest or clashes of personality. In this session and the following one, we will look at ways of dealing with these more difficult situations.

DISAGREEMENTS

When you strongly disagree with someone, it is hard to maintain a good working relationship. The disagreement becomes the focus of the attention of both parties, and it is easy to lose sight of the human beings involved. What's more, we tend to equate the disagreement to the person – 'You're wrong' – rather than separate them out – 'I disagree with your opinion'. So how do we use people skills to deal with conflict more effectively?

AVOIDING CONFLICT

The first thing to consider is whether you can prevent the situation from becoming one of conflict.

PREPARING YOURSELF

I have already suggested that you set up your intentions and outcomes before you begin an interaction (see Chapter 6). These will give you a positive frame for the situation. I have also suggested that you get yourself ready to be constructive and positive in the situation. (See Chapter 2.)

MAKING THE OTHER READY

You can use these same techniques with the other person before you start into the task or meeting, to make it more likely that you avoid conflict.

Start by checking out what state they are in. Many conflicts start because someone is feeling negative in the first place, as a result of something that has happened beforehand. Remind the person of good encounters you have had, or give them some space to improve their state. Perhaps you can find a way of encouraging them to make themselves feel good – a treat.

AGREEING INTENTION AND OUTCOMES

If they are feeling negative about the present interaction, you can often change that by talking about your intention and preferred outcomes for the meeting. You can then ask them to describe how they would like the meeting to go, and see if you can come to an agreement about the intention and outcomes.

It is very rare for someone to express a negative outcome for a meeting, like, 'I want us to disagree and fail to come to a decision'. By asking them how they would like the meeting to go, you are encouraging them to find a positive outcome and express it.

Scenario – Finding a positive outcome

Andrew went to meet with David about the approach they would take to the project they were going to do together. The former came to the meeting in a foul mood. He had just had another project given to him by their manager, increasing his work-load yet more, and he was already sure that he and David tackled things differently and wouldn't agree on a way of working.

David spotted straight away that Andrew was not in a good state for this meeting. He asked Andrew how he was, and Andrew replied, 'Not good.'

David asked, 'What's been happening?'

Andrew explained about the new project and that he felt overloaded. David suggested that they could sort this out quickly and have one task out of the way. He went on to say that he wanted them to find an approach they were both comfortable with, and that he wanted to do so by open discussion of their differences. He then asked what Andrew wanted out of the meeting.

Andrew said, 'I don't want to waste my time.' 'So what *do* you want?' asked David gently. 'The same as you, I guess,' said Andrew. 'I just want to feel that we can work constructively and effectively together, and to have agreed the way we'll do that.' The situation was now off to a better start.

YOUR REACTION

If your reaction to a potential conflict is to become defensive or aggressive – to take up the message of conflict and respond to it – then conflict is inevitable.

On the other hand, if you continue to maintain a positive and constructive state, you may be able to defuse the conflict before it begins. Remembering your intention and outcomes will help you to do this, as will reminders of constructive meetings you have had.

Just be aware of your own body posture and keep it relaxed. Remember, too, your voice tone. Don't allow it to become harsh, keep your voice soft and friendly.

PHYSICAL POSITIONING

You can also help to avoid conflict if you avoid the type of physical positioning that encourages it. This may sound too simplistic as a technique, but, in fact, we automatically make these adjustments when we are in a good state, and they **do** make a difference. Make sure that your seat or standing position is relatively close to the other person, and that you are literally on the same side as them. Make sure that neither of you towers above the other.

It is harder to have conflict if you are both seated on the same side of the table, or you are standing facing the same flip chart.

If it is not possible to achieve this, at least go some way towards it. Stand if they are standing, sit if they are sitting. If you are on opposite sides of a table, and you do not feel you can move round, at least reposition your chair, so that you are at an angle to them, not directly opposite.

These may seem like trivial points, but they are remarkably useful in helping to change the tone of a situation. Next time you are in an argument at home, try it out!

NOTICING WHAT'S HAPPENING

There is often the possibility of avoiding conflict by noticing what's happening before it gets out of hand, and doing something about it. Disagreements need not lead to conflict – they can lead to useful discussions and improved under-standing of different viewpoints. It is all about attitudes you adopt to the situation.

Exercise 40 – Avoiding conflict

Think of a typical conflict situation that you have been in, and work out how you could have avoided the conflict constructively.

From the ideas you have had individually, as a group, list up on the flip chart the strategies you could use to avoid the situation becoming a conflict in the first place.

DEALING WITH CONFLICT

Sometimes, however, the conflict is there without you being able to catch it before it develops. So what can you do to deal with it once it's already become a conflict?

STEPPING BACK

The first thing you need to do when caught up in a conflict situation is to detach yourself from the emotional turbulence and imagine that you are observing what's happening.

YOUR OWN STATE

Start by checking out what state you are in. Remind yourself of times when you have handled a conflict of interest well.

Remind yourself of positive encounters you have had with this person. Calm your breathing and relax your body posture.

All of this will only take a couple of moments. You can do it on the spot, or you might choose to take time out of the meeting to regain a more useful state of mind. (For more on how to do this, see Chapter 2.)

THE CONFLICT ENVIRONMENT

Once you have calmed yourself down a little, you can notice if the set-up of the room, or the physical positioning of yourself in relation to the other, are perpetuating the state of conflict.

By making changes in positioning and posture you can calm the atmosphere down, and make it easier to deal with the disagreement more constructively.

Scenario — Calming the conflict

Paul approached Sue, already raging at what he believed she had said about him. He caught her unawares, and she began to spring to her defence. Then she stopped a moment, and stepped back in her imagination from the situation. She noticed that she looked as angry as him. She calmed herself down, and remembered that usually they got on quite well. She then noticed that they were both standing up and facing each other. She suggested that they sat down and talked about it properly, and deliberately softened her voice to remove the anger.

Paul agreed to sit down, and was already calming down a bit himself.

WHAT IS THE CONFLICT ABOUT?

Having taken these initial steps to cool the conflict situation, you can begin to sort out exactly what the conflict is about.

MISUNDERSTANDING

Sometimes conflict arises because of a misunderstanding. Someone didn't listen carefully to a message, or interpreted it differently from someone else.

Rather than recognize the misunderstanding for what it is, we often get caught up in the argument about who interpreted correctly, and who interpreted wrongly, and lose sight of the real issue, which is how to find a **common** understanding.

If it is your message that was misinterpreted, then you need to find a way of communicating it differently, so that you both agree. It is not useful to blame the other person for not understanding. It is far more useful to have another go at explaining it.

If you are the one who has misunderstood, it is not useful to blame the other person for not communicating effectively. It is far more useful to ask them to explain it again, and check whether you are now understanding correctly by giving them your own version.

If you have both interpreted someone else's message differently, then you need to check out your different interpretations without telling each other, 'You're wrong'. If necessary, you may need to go back to the source of the message, and ask them to have another go.

DIFFERENT APPROACHES

Sometimes conflict arises because you have different ways of doing something.

Scenario – Dealing with different approaches

Terry and June had to prepare a presentation to the team together. Terry wanted to start by preparing the OHTs. June wanted to start by making notes of what they would say.

Terry   My previous manager told me always to get my materials together first.

June	Well, I always think about what I want to say first.
Terry	But that's wrong.
June	Who says your old manager was right?
Terry	Well, it works.
June	So does my way.

Neither person was considering the other's approach as even a possibility. The argument was destroying the potential for constructive preparation, and was ready to spin out of control.

In this sort of situation, you need to stop to take stock of the alternatives. First you want to find out how the preferred approach works for the other person: 'What is it about doing it in that way that you find useful?' Then explain your preferred approach: 'I prefer to do it this way, because I find that ...'.

Now you can negotiate about how you both agree to tackle it, with some understanding of what matters to the other person.

DIFFERENT INTERESTS

Another area in which we can have conflict is the area of our interests, which means what we want to get out of the situation.

One person may want to impress the boss, while the other is more concerned about just getting the task finished – they have different interests. This will influence the approach the person wants to take, and how they view the task itself, and needs to be recognized as the root cause of the conflict.

Again, the best way to deal with this is to find out exactly what the other person wants out of the situation, to explain what you want, and to negotiate a way of meeting the interests of both as far as you can. I have already talked about checking out intention and outcomes as a way of avoiding conflict. If you already have the conflict, then go back to that again: 'What exactly do you want to get out of doing this?'

DIFFERENT VALUES

Sometimes the conflict arises because the two parties concerned have different core values. The stereotypical examples of this are discussions on politics and religion, where both parties believe they are right. However, it also occurs in many apparently ordinary work situations.

Scenario – Different core values

Gill and Pete were discussing how to approach a project they were doing. Pete suggested that he would prepare rough notes on it, and Gill could expand them on the word processor into the final report.

Gill was furious. She saw this as suggesting that she wasn't capable of thinking up the initial ideas, and was only capable of word processing – a woman's job. She felt insulted and demeaned and told Pete in no uncertain terms what she felt.

He was astounded. He had seen it as a fair division of labour, which would enable them to do it without too much hassle. He also knew that Gill was more efficient than he was at finishing things well, so thought it made sense to split up the work that way. What he had failed to do was to take account of the fact that Gill felt very strongly about the role of women in the workplace.

When someone feels that your proposal is unfair, or reacts with strong negative feelings, then the likelihood is that you are seen as expressing strong values or beliefs that go against theirs. By being more aware of their values, you can avoid causing this type of conflict. (See Chapter 5.)

It is bad enough when you accidentally upset someone, because you have been insensitive to what matters to them, as in the above example. It is more difficult to deal with if you genuinely hold values that oppose theirs. If, in the example above, Pete thought that women **should** play a subsidiary role, and **weren't** capable of having ideas, then the conflict would be far worse.

In more philosophical discussions, you may simply have to agree to disagree. You can respect another person's opinion or point of view without agreeing with them. By treating their opinion with respect, you will usually find that they will do the same to you, and you can leave the conflict arena. However, if the values that are conflicting have implications for how you work together, then you have to deal with the conflict. The only way out of it is to find some value or belief that you both share, which is more important to you both than the area of conflict. This might be doing the task successfully, or getting on well with others, or having a peaceful life, or, of course, many other possibilities.

You then have something you agree about to start from, and can negotiate a way around the conflict. This doesn't mean to say you ignore the area of disagreement. It means that you start from some common ground in the discussion, and thereby take a more positive approach to the area of disagreement.

You may suggest a value that you could agree on to the other person, or you may ask them: 'What do you think we both feel that is important enough to take us past this disagreement?' or 'What would be important enough to you to allow you to find a way past this conflict?'

Of course, you will first have to ask yourself a similar question. If you haven't given yourself a good reason to come past the conflict first, you certainly won't convince the other person.

CONFLICT OF PERSONALITY

This is the most difficult area of conflict to overcome. If I don't like you, or you don't like me, then it is very difficult to relate well together, and we will find almost any excuse to be in conflict.

I would suggest that, if you find yourself in this predicament, the first tactic should be avoidance of situations where you have to relate and work together.

It is important to recognize that this type of clash **is** very difficult to overcome, and that it may be more practical to avoid situations where you are in contact with each other as much as possible. You can admit to it as a problem, but deal with it practically, and will often be able to address it in this way.

Scenario – We don't like each other

John had been asked to accept Julie into his project team. He knew that Julie didn't like him and that the contact between them tended to lead to conflict. They were both strong characters, and although he had tried to find ways to deal with her more effectively, whatever he did or said seemed to be like a red rag to a bull.

He went to his manager and stated the problem. He said that he had not yet succeeded in finding a way of making the relationship easier between himself and Julie, and that he was concerned that it would cause problems in the project team, not just for them, but for the others. His manager agreed to place Julie elsewhere, and suggested that John continue to try to find ways of improving the relationship.

Sometimes, however, it is inevitable that the two of you will have to work together, so you need to find a way to try to avoid being tempted into conflict.

You need to ask yourself the question: 'What is more important to me than the clash of personality with this person?' You can then find something to relate to in that person. Examples might be:

- I don't like this person, but they do get the job done quickly and efficiently, and I can benefit from that in working with them.

- We don't get on with each other, but we do both want to do our work well and get recognition for that.
- We don't like each other, but I don't want to give the impression that I'm behaving like children in the playground who are 'enemies'. I want to show that I can deal with this in a mature way.

Then you can focus on the outcomes you both want in whatever you are undertaking, by clarifying your own, and asking about theirs.

By deciding to make it work, and focusing on what helps to make it work, you can shift your attention from the personality clash. And often you find that they're not so disagreeable as you thought! We are all a mixture of characteristics, and if you concentrate on dealing constructively with the individual, you often elicit some of their more constructive characteristics.

Exercise 41 – Action to calm conflict

Think of a conflict situation that you have experienced recently. Identify what the conflict was about. Now note down what you could have done about it (Figure 10.1).

Type of conflict	Actions I could have taken

FIGURE 10.1 The conflict table

Compare your ideas in the whole group.

USE OF LANGUAGE

Whatever the reason for the conflict, we very quickly adopt conflict language, and thereby maintain the conflict situation. There are two types of conflict language, and both can be consciously changed.

CONFLICT METAPHOR

The first type is when we talk 'battle talk'. We describe the other person as if they were our enemy. We describe the situation as 'conflict', 'battle of wills', 'fight to the death'. We describe ourselves or the other person as 'wounded', 'beaten', 'triumphant', and so on.

This type of language sets us up for a battle, and indicates that there will be a winner and a loser. By changing the language, we can change the situation. If we look at how we can both gain from the interchange, if we look for what we share as common values, we begin to shift from battle talk to constructive peace talk.

PERSONALITY LANGUAGE

The other way we maintain conflict through our language is by personalizing our comments.

- 'You make me angry.'
- 'You're wrong.'
- 'You don't understand.'
- 'Don't be stupid.'

When we do this, we take the conflict immediately to a personality level – the most difficult to deal with. It is important to identify that it is behaviour or a problem that is causing the conflict usually, not a person as a whole. Better ways of expressing this are:

- 'I am angry about x.'
- 'I don't agree with what you're saying.'
- 'I haven't made myself clear to you.'
- 'You seem to be missing the point I'm trying to make.'

We still express our feelings, but we don't blame the other person for them. The former set of statements leads to: 'No, you're wrong'. The latter set of statements opens the path for further discussions or clarification.

Exercise 42 – Alternative use of language

As a group, brainstorm on to a flip chart, on the lefthand side, typical battle talk and personalized statements.

Now come up with alternatives that are more constructive, and fill them in on the righthand side.

TAKING ACTION

In all conflict situations, you make a positive difference if you choose to do something about it, rather than allow it to grow. Most conflicts are minor in the first place, but because both sides react by rising to the conflict, they grow disproportionately. If you step back, you can stop that growth, and deal constructively with the issue. This is often easier to do if you are not one of the parties involved. You are already one step back from the situation, and can see what's happening more clearly. It is worth while practising our skills at changing conflict when we are outside the situation, so that we become better at handling it when we are involved.

CONCLUSION

Conflict is the negative side of something that is useful. It happens when we pick up on the negativity and allow it to become predominant.

However, total avoidance of disagreement would be equally unhealthy. If no one ever expresses a difference of opinion or viewpoint, there is no development of new ideas or new approaches, and we need that development.

What we need is the skill of dealing with divergent views constructively, so that we can all gain from them, rather than come out of it feeling battle-weary.

ACTION LIST – USING PEOPLE SKILLS IN DEALING WITH CONFLICT

1. Think about a situation in the near future where there could be conflict between you and someone else. Find a way to avoid the conflict.
2. Next time you see conflict between two members of the team, stop what's happening, encourage them to step back, and find a way of resolving the conflict.
3. Next time you are in a conflict situation, stop for a moment, and see if you can resolve it.

CHAPTER 11

DEALING WITH DIFFICULT PEOPLE

KEY LEARNING POINTS

- assuming they won't be difficult
- using self-management
- reclassifying difficult as different
- dealing with emotional behaviour
- dealing with difficult personality traits
- dealing with communication difficulties

NOTES TO MANAGER/COACH

Remember to check through the relevant chapters referred to in this one, to make sure that you remember the parts I'm referring to, and can remind the team if necessary.

INTRODUCTION

All the material we have covered until now reduces the need for specific strategies to deal with difficult people, because you won't come across so many in that category. That may sound strange to you. Let me explain.

As we become more skilful at relating to others, they are less likely to display their 'difficult' side. If we set ourselves up well, and respond to their differences constructively, they will respond more positively to us, and we will find them easier to deal with.

We usually underestimate the influence we can have on others, and don't realize that how we behave affects how they behave. I have often had people who have been on training programmes with me report back that their team or their customers have improved, so it's now easier to relate to them. I always laugh, and say, 'Well done!' And they will still sometimes deny that it's anything to do with them.

However, we do all come across people who are being difficult some of the time, and in this chapter we look at ways of dealing with typical difficult characters.

YOUR EXPECTATIONS

Many of the people you encounter have a reputation. That means that someone has told you what they are like, or you have previous experience of dealing with them. If the reputation is a good one – that they are friendly or helpful – it is useful, because you automatically assume that they will be like that with you in the next encounter. This assumption sets you up physically and mentally for a useful encounter, and the likelihood is that it will be a self-fulfilling prophecy.

On the other hand, if the person is known to be difficult, then your assumption may be that they will be difficult for you to deal with. This could be another self-fulfilling prophecy. We tend to get what we expect, so beware!

The good news is that you can change this story. You simply have to decide to expect something more constructive, and act on the assumption that they will be co-operative, and you will have a useful interaction. By deliberately setting yourself up with expectations of a useful encounter, you change how you are physically and mentally, and thereby change the person's response to you. (See Chapters 3 and 6 for more on this.)

Scenario – Making a different assumption

John was asked to deal with a particular supplier, because Mary, who usually dealt with her, was off work ill. His colleagues commiserated with him. They were relieved that it wasn't them, because everyone knew that this supplier was really difficult to deal with.

She had no manners, she was argumentative, and she always laid the blame for any problems firmly with the other party.

At first, John agreed with his colleagues that he was in for a difficult time. He had heard the tales about her as well. Then he remembered that Mary didn't complain about her. He decided that it might be possible to produce a different effect.

He thought about the meeting, and decided to act as if she were friendly and helpful, like a particular supplier he often dealt with. He checked through in his mind how he wanted the meeting to go, and what actions he wanted from it.

When Mrs Jones arrived, he greeted her pleasantly and offered her a cup of coffee. She smiled and said, 'Yes, please, I've been stuck in a traffic jam for half an hour, and it's really frustrating.' He sympathized, fetched a drink, and they sat down together and began the meeting.

Exercise 43 – Dealing with difficult behaviour

Think of someone you find difficult to deal with. Note down the characteristics that make them difficult.

Now think of how you would like them to be. Note down the different behaviours. Who do you know who is like this?

Imagine that, in your next encounter with the person that you have found difficult, they are like the other person who is easy to relate to. What would **you** do differently? Note down how **you** would change.

Now imagine how the next encounter could be, with you behaving differently, and the other person reacting differently.
Talk in the whole group about what you noticed.

This strategy won't always work, but it gives a better chance of a useful interaction, because others react unconsciously to how we are. If we deal with them as if they are going to relate well to us, often they do.

YOUR STATE

What the above strategy also does is set you up to be positive and constructive. This is very important, because we all deal more effectively with difficult people when we are in a good state ourselves.

You can do some extra work on your own physical and mental state, to make yourself even more ready to deal effectively with the individual. By using the techniques described in Chapter 2, you can make sure that you are 'on form', and therefore find it easier to deal with the individual.

You know that when you're feeling a bit 'off' it is more difficult for you to relate well to **anyone**, so it makes sense to make a special effort to prepare yourself for dealing with someone you don't automatically relate well to.

Exercise 44 – Being ready in yourself

Remember yourself now in an encounter that you found easy and useful. Notice how you are, physically and mentally. Think of things that help you to get into this state, besides the expectation of a good encounter.

Examples

- being dressed comfortably in clothes you like
- going for a short walk beforehand
- reminding yourself of times when you have related well to others

Make your own list, and share it with two other people in the team – you might prompt each other to have more ideas!

You can use the strategies for self-management both before the interaction and during it. If you find yourself in the middle of a difficult situation, take a moment or two, and regain for yourself a useful state. Don't allow someone else's behaviour to turn you into a difficult person to deal with.

RESPECTING DIFFERENCES

When we are dealing with somebody we find difficult, we often play a part in causing them to be that way, because we label them as such. Rather than seeing them as being different, we judge them to be difficult. This sets both us and them up to find problems.

If, instead, we noticed that the person was different, and spent a little time finding out about their differences, we might find them easier to deal with! By discovering what matters to them, and relating what we have to say to their priorities or values, we may avoid the problem. (For more on this, see Chapter 5.)

IT'S STILL DIFFICULT

So far, I've suggested that you can make a difference to the so-called difficult people you have to deal with, by preparing yourself well for the interaction, by setting up a different expectation in yourself, and by finding out about their differences and working to those.

However, I wouldn't expect this to clear away one hundred per cent of the difficulties in relating to others. There will still be times when you find people difficult.

There are many categories of 'types' we find difficult to deal with, and what I propose to do is to go through some of the most common ones, and suggest strategies that might help.

ARGUMENTATIVE

There are some people who seem to delight in playing the devil's advocate. No matter what the subject, they find a way of offering a contrary view on it, and object on principle to any idea put forward. This can be infuriating in the wrong context. However, the first thing to remember is that, in the right context, such a person can be very useful.

Scenario – Using the argumentative person well

Chris and Jackie had prepared a new proforma for a particular process. They wanted it to be accepted by those who had to use it, so they needed someone to check it out from the point of view of the customer. Chris suggested they ask Mark, because he was always playing devil's advocate in their team meetings.

They went to Mark, and Chris said: 'Mark, you are really good at spotting what won't work, and we wondered if you would help us by checking this proforma through from a customer's perspective, and then tell us what we need to amend.'

Mark was surprised and pleased to be asked, and did so conscientiously. He returned the proforma to them, and rather than just identifying what was wrong, he made a couple of suggestions for improvements.

If you use this quality in others, when it does suit the context, they are less likely to apply it when it isn't useful. We all want to be recognized for what we can do, and most behaviours do have some context in which they are useful.

However, if the person is being argumentative in an inappropriate context, you need to find a way to change their reaction. Otherwise you will get caught up in the 'I'm right, you're wrong' syndrome. Normally we are told to deal with objections as they come up, but you know that if someone is being argumentative, they will continue to find more and more objections, and it is very hard to keep going constructively.

The quickest way I know to make this change is to ask the person themselves what would make the difference.

Examples of appropriate questions are:

■ 'What would make it possible for you to agree this point?'
■ 'What would resolve that problem, in your opinion?'

The answers to questions like these usually give you information that allows you to negotiate an agreement.

AGGRESSIVE

A step up from the argumentative person is someone who is being downright aggressive. In this situation, you can feel personally threatened, as opposed to just feeling that your ideas are being rejected.

When someone is being aggressive, you need to change the whole tone of the proceedings. The problem is more than just the subject matter. The vital first step is to ensure that you are in control of your own state. Use the techniques we have already explored to help yourself to stay calm and detached. There is a real danger of being drawn into behaviour that is either equally aggressive, or defensive, and neither of these help the situation.

When you have taken a step back, and regained a good state for yourself, you can assess the state of the other person. There are two strategies that can be effective in calming them down, and you may have to experiment to see which one works.

1. *Opposite behaviour* When someone is aggressive, they are usually physically agitated, loud and harsh in their voice tone, and forceful in their body posture. If you are calm and still, and talk quietly yet firmly, you can often bring them down to a quieter form of behaviour.
2. *Complementary behaviour* Sometimes your calmness will make them even worse. When that happens, you need to match them, without the aggression. Again, you make yourself calm, but this time, you address them quite loudly and firmly, and literally stand firm to do so. You can then gradually become quieter and less forceful, and they will also calm down.

These strategies will take the heat out of the situation, so that you can explore the reason behind the aggressive behaviour, and look for something that is more constructive. This is important. Remember that when someone is habitually aggressive, they have usually found that it works for them as a behaviour. By not playing the other side of the game, you can change that, and maybe help them to find a better way of getting what they want out of the situation.

If it is unusual for them to be aggressive, it is likely to be because something has crossed their boundaries of what they can accept, and you need to discover what that is.

Once the person has calmed down a little, you can discover what has caused the behaviour, by asking, 'What has caused you to have such a strong reaction?' or 'How can we deal with this issue constructively?'

ANGRY

Aggressive behaviour often happens because someone is angry. However, anger is not always demonstrated by aggression. Some people hold their anger back, and become like pressure cookers, with the anger bubbling away inside them.

By standing back a little, we can all spot the signs of anger, whether it's overt or covert, and it is important to deal with it directly, because otherwise it may cause even more difficult behaviour.

When someone is angry, it is usually because we have said or done something that offends their personal value system – or someone else has and we are feeling the effects. The first step is to acknowledge their anger, and show that you have noticed. It is important to state this acknowledgement carefully. Anger is a very strong emotion and tends to be directed personally: 'You make me angry by ...'. Such statements condemn, and make us feel angry or hurt in response, and we need to maintain control of our own state.

Scenario – Dealing with anger

Maggie just smiled when Doug said that she was ignoring his point. He reacted angrily, saying she always did that, just dismissed what he had to say.

Maggie said, 'What has happened to make you feel angry?'

No one listens to me or takes me seriously,' said Doug, 'yet I've more experience of this than any of you.'

By acknowledging the anger, Maggie has discovered what lies behind it, and now can do something about it. By asking a question which **doesn't** indicate that she took the anger as a personal attack, she elicits a more useful answer.

Having acknowledged the anger, you immediately release its pressure a little, and can now find out what would release it more. Anger comes from feeling personally devalued in some way – our feelings or our values seem to be ignored or stepped on.

If I want to relate well with this person, I will need to be more considerate of these feelings or values, even if I don't agree with them. Again, if I'm not sure what would work, I tend to ask the person directly: 'What can I do that would make you feel that I respected your viewpoint?'

It is important to remember that often it is not your particular behaviour that has created the anger. It is a cumulative thing, and your behaviour just happens to have triggered it. We have all experienced the situation where something has made us angry at work, and we've concealed it. Then we go home and a loved one says or does the wrong thing, and gets the cumulative blast of our day's anger, for a relatively minor issue.

By acknowledging that the person is angry, without taking it personally, we can often defuse the situation, and help them to clear the anger, and find a more constructive path through the issue.

HURT OR UPSET

The other side of anger is hurt. While some people react to feeling devalued by being angry, others react by being hurt. This can be equally difficult to deal with, as the person is likely to withdraw into their shell and become unapproachable.

In this situation, you need first of all to give recognition to their state, as you do with anger. This may sound simple, but frequently our reaction is to act as if the other person is all right, because we find their hurt difficult to deal with.

Just by saying, 'I can see that you're feeling upset/hurt', we give the person an important acknowledgement. It is important to say this with respect for their state. That means being calm and fairly quiet, rather than trying to bounce them out of it.

Beware, though, of the danger of becoming so attuned to their state that you join them! You must stay detached to be able to be useful in the interaction, otherwise there are two of you feeling upset or hurt, and someone else will have to help you to become more positive.

After acknowledging their state, you can move on to finding out what has caused the reaction. Again, ask your question carefully: 'What has happened to make you feel this way?' By encouraging the person to express a little of what they are feeling, you will help them to release the intensity of feeling, so that they have more chance of moving into a more useful state. Remember, too, to make no judgement about what they say. They want sympathy and recognition, not opinions. It is then possible to ask them what would make them feel better about the situation, and you will have useful information to help them move into a more useful encounter.

Remember that the reason we tend to withdraw if we are hurt or upset is that we fear that we are vulnerable. If another human being is calm and sympathetic with us, we will feel less vulnerable, and begin to open up again.

SHY

Sometimes people are withdrawn, not because of a specific upset, but because that is their nature. Again, it is a symptom of feeling vulnerable and unsure of themselves, and it is their way of protecting themselves.

Once someone who is shy feels safe with you, they will open up more, so your priority is to create a safe environment.

Make sure that you are physically positioned so that you are non-threatening – be seated, and open and relaxed in your posture. Speak gently and talk about things that they know about and feel comfortable with. Encourage them to relax in their posture, and maybe even to laugh! Then you can gradually move towards the conversation you want to have.

With all the above characteristics, you are dealing with people's emotions. It is important to recognize this, and keep yourself in a positive and detached state, using the techniques we have already covered, so that you don't get caught up in their state.

By respecting their state, and recognizing it, you can often help them to move to something more useful.

With the following characteristics, you are dealing more with personality traits. These are more difficult, because when we find such traits hard to handle, it indicates a clash of values. This requires a slightly different approach.

DISAGREEABLE

When someone is just being unpleasant, it can be very difficult. We tend to decide that they are 'that sort of person', and switch off, or react with negative emotions. It can help if you remember that very few people are disagreeable all the time. It is usually a passing phase, rather than a permanent attribute, and even if they are often in an unpleasant mood, they are sometimes in a good one!

So the most useful way forward is to act as if they are being agreeable! By not reacting to their being disagreeable, you can often change the behaviour.

It can also be useful to notice or find out what changes their mood to something more pleasant:

■ Are they someone who is easier to deal with in the afternoon/morning?

- Are they someone who is easier to deal with if they haven't just come out of a meeting?
- Are they someone who is easier to deal with outside the work environment?
- Are they someone who is easier to deal with individually rather than in a group?

We can make the interaction easier for ourselves by identifying possible strategies to catch them in a better mood!

BIGOTED

Sometimes the way in which someone is disagreeable indicates that they are bigoted, and that their prejudice counteracts your core values. For example, the person may express racist or sexist views or behaviour that you find offensive.

In this situation, it is important not to compromise your own values, and at the same time not to get into an argument about whose values are right and whose are wrong. (See Chapter 10 for more on this.)

You may feel that you are able to move the discussion to a different level, where the conflicting values do not get in the way, or you may feel that you need to confront the bigotry. When we confront bigotry, it is very important to do so in a way that is constructive. I would suggest the following form of words:

'I do not like the way you talk about/are behaving with x. It implies sexism/racism to me, and I find it offensive. That means that I find it hard to deal with you constructively, and I would like to be able to move past this block.'

Notice that, by using a statement like this, you would not be accusing the bigot – you would simply be stating your own feelings. This would allow the bigot to move from their position, because you had not attacked them. You might even suggest ways of moving by telling the bigot what would make you feel more comfortable with the situation.

If you are the direct recipient of their bigotry, be careful not to become the 'victim'. It is important that you maintain your state of self-esteem and self-belief. Use the techniques from Chapter 2 to help you.

CONDESCENDING

Sometimes there is not an obvious bigotry in the other person, but they do seem condescending or arrogant towards you. The immediate reaction to such behaviour tends to be either to become subjective, as if they had reason to be so, or to become angry, because you feel devalued.

It is more useful to react to them as an equal, and to maintain a calm and confident state.

Scenario – Dealing with condescension

Lisa had been in her post for two months, while Steve had been doing the job for 29 years. Lisa's report-back on her project at the team meeting seemed to have been received well. Afterwards Steve said to her, 'Well, Lisa, another five years and you should be able to do this job quite well.'

Lisa's immediate reaction was to feel angry at his condescension, but then she took a deep breath. She needed to be able to work with Steve, and gain his respect and co-operation. 'You're right,' she said. 'We're all on a learning curve here. Even being in the job for 29 years doesn't guarantee that you'll always get it right, does it!'

Steve looked a bit taken aback, and immediately defended his own expertise.

'Oh, of course your experience is valuable, Steve', said Lisa, 'just as my background in information technology is.'

By staying pleasant and in control, Lisa was able to counteract the condescension without causing a worsening of the relationship.

STUPID

Sometimes the problem with someone else is not their arrogance, it's their stupidity! We are sometimes in danger of being the person who is condescending, because the other person seems to us to be being stupid or foolish.

In this situation, we need to stop and take stock. First, we need to remember what it feels like to be treated as stupid or foolish – we have all experienced it at some time or another. This reminds us that you don't elicit useful behaviour from someone by treating them as if they are stupid.

Second, we need to consider the reason for the behaviour. It could be that:

1. They have not understood your message correctly.
2. They have a valid reason for believing they are right.
3. It's a way of getting attention.

We can now try out strategies to deal with each of these possible reasons.

THEY HAVE NOT UNDERSTOOD YOUR MESSAGE CORRECTLY

In this case, take responsibility. Turn it around to, 'I have not communicated my message effectively', and have another go in a different way.

THEY HAVE A VALID REASON FOR BELIEVING THEY ARE RIGHT

In this case, find out their viewpoint, what is causing them to maintain their position. After all, they may indeed have a valid reason, and if you still don't think so, you will at least know what you have to convince them about.

IT'S A WAY OF GETTING ATTENTION

By giving real attention, we can dissolve this one. See Chapter 4 for more information on this.

The above characteristics are usually the most difficult to deal with because they are so linked to personality. However, there is a final set of characteristics that we find hard because they are about the way in which people communicate.

PEOPLE WHO DON'T LISTEN

There is nothing more frustrating than trying to communicate with someone who isn't listening to you – it's a frequent cause of domestic rows! What we really mean by this is that we want them to give attention and/or we want them to act on the communication. So it is useful to be explicit about what we want, so that they know.

Scenario – Asking for attention

Bob was convinced that June never listened to what he had to say. He decided to do something about it in their next encounter.

He started by saying to June that he needed her attention for a few minutes, and asked her if she could spare the time now. She said she could, and stopped what she was doing – a useful first step.

Then he said that he wanted to know whether she had grasped his point, as it was important to him to have a result on this. He said he would appreciate it if she would tell him what she was going to do about their discussion, and he would tell her what he was going to do.

She smiled and said, 'So long as we both have to do something, it makes sense to me, I agree.' He had definitely made a good start.

Remember that often the reason why people don't listen is that they don't think that it's particularly relevant for them. You can introduce something that **is** relevant to them to catch their attention. Even if their reason for not listening is that they are busy thinking about what **they** want to say, this technique will still work.

PEOPLE WHO TALK TOO MUCH

These are often the same people who don't listen because they are too busy thinking about what they have to say! If you can't get a word in edgeways, then you need to find ways of interrupting their flow that draw their attention.

There are two I would recommend. First, use physical movement. This doesn't mean fidgeting. People who talk too much can ignore that. I mean a substantial shift in your physical positioning. Stand up and move to the window. Move your chair closer or further away from them. This substantial movement draws their attention to you, and gives a space for you to come in.

Second, use a different voice tone. (You could also address them by name – this unconsciously tends to remind people of school, and stops them.) Speak loudly and firmly, or even speak very softly. By changing your way of speaking, you will again draw their attention and give yourself some space.

Remember that most people who talk too much don't intend to block you out, they are just caught up in their own story.

PEOPLE WHO WAFFLE

Similar to the above category are those who talk and never seem to get to the point. With these I would use the same techniques as above, but add to them a question, such as: 'So what exactly do you want me to do?' or 'So what exactly do you want to tell me?' or 'So how exactly will this affect us?'

Exercise 45 – Using strategies to deal with difficult people

In pairs, try dealing with someone who is being difficult. Choose a characteristic from those listed, and be like that – you may use as your model someone you have found difficult. Agree a scenario with your partner, and now let them experiment with how to deal more effectively with you. (Use the notes on the different characteristics to help.) Then reverse roles and let them be the difficult person. Have some fun doing this!

THE ESSENTIAL STRATEGIES

I have gone through some of the more common behaviours that we find difficult to deal with. I would hope that applying the techniques we have looked at in earlier chapters would reduce the number of times you encounter a real difficulty. When you do, remember that there are two essential strategies to bear in mind:

1. Managing your own state.
2. Remembering the person behind the behaviour.

MANAGING YOUR OWN STATE

The more you practise the techniques to prepare yourself for interactions with others, the less likely you are to get caught up in their games.

It is vital to be able to step back and notice what's happening, so that you can do something about it. By being in a good state yourself, and by staying detached and clear about wanting a useful outcome, you make this easier for yourself.

REMEMBERING THE PERSON BEHIND THE BEHAVIOUR

Whatever someone does or doesn't do is just their behaviour at this moment. We all have our ups and downs in the way we relate to each other, and it is important to maintain your perspective.

By continuing to respond to the best in someone, we often succeed in bringing out those more useful characteristics. No one really wants, deep down, to have poor relationships with others. If you can help someone to find a more useful way of behaving, you are doing them a favour, as well as yourself!

ACTION LIST – DEALING WITH DIFFICULT PEOPLE

1. Experiment with someone who has been difficult for you in the past, by acting as if this time they will be easy to relate to.
2. Stop using the word 'difficult' in relation to people.
3. Experiment with the strategies on two types of difficulty that you encounter in the next two weeks.
4. Agree as a team to challenge each other if you are being difficult, so that you recognize the traits clearly.

CHAPTER 12

CONCLUSION

Writing about how to develop your people skills really makes you stop to think. Over the period of time I have spent putting this book together, I have become more and more aware of just how important these skills are.

- I notice that one of the reasons that I use my corner shop so much is that the staff in there always greet me in a friendly way, and have a conversation with me, as opposed to just serving me.
- I notice that the managers who really achieve things with their teams are those who treat their staff as special people.
- I notice that the people who enjoy their work are all people who make good relationships with others.

This topic is not an added extra, to be considered if you have some spare time. It is central to effective working.

We are entering an area at work where people will be the crucial factor in making the difference to how a company thrives. I think they always were, but it is becoming more and more obvious as we approach the twenty-first century. None of the systems and processes that can lead to improved work practice will be effective unless the people involved are committed to making them work, and even improving them. That commitment comes when people feel valued and happy in their work. And much of that sense of feeling valued will come from an ethos where people skills **are** seen as important.

This is not something that can be imposed – everyone can help to make this difference in the workplace, by deciding to treat everyone else as they would wish to be treated. Good relationships are infectious: if you make the effort, others are likely to reciprocate.

The material in this book all relates to everyday working practice. None of it is new, because all of it only describes what people do naturally when they are in a good state. So I have offered you a chance to remind yourself of what common sense tells us anyway.

The problem lies with the development of the habit of using our common sense. It is not something that most of us have been encouraged to do! We all know that we relate better to others when we are feeling good ourselves; we all know that other people can be easy to relate to if we bother to find out how to handle them well; and we all know that working life is easier and more effective if we relate well with others. Yet this knowing has not led automatically to giving priority to developing our people skills. Instead we continue to fit in with the present work ethos of trying to get everything done, and to meet targets, seeing people as yet another hindrance to our efficiency.

It does not take long to make the difference that helps us to break through to a more effective way of working with others. You will notice that in the action points, I have usually suggested that you experiment with applying the techniques we have covered in one or two situations, to begin to give yourself the habit, without simultaneously giving yourself a headache. I would propose that you continue to practise some of the techniques in this way, gradually re-educating yourself into a more useful way of dealing with others.

It is also important to accept that we all get it wrong sometimes. When you notice that you **haven't** applied the practice in some interaction, begin by congratulating yourself on noticing. Before, you would probably have just blamed the other person! One of my teachers suggested that I bought myself a flower every time I noticed that I had 'failed'. It was an excellent way of stopping me from engaging in self-blame, and turning my attention to how I could improve the situation.

So the second stage of action when you notice 'failure' is simply to ask yourself what you would do differently next time you are in a similar situation. As you think of some change you could make, rehearse it through in your mind, and you will set yourself up to react differently the next time.

You can significantly speed up the process of developing your people skills by agreeing as a group that you are going to help each other and reinforce good practice. You will notice that I have suggested several ways of doing this in the action points, and I am sure that you can think of others. By contracting together to notice good practice, and to prompt it where it slips in each other, you will develop the habit far more quickly, and you can have some fun while doing so.

No matter what you do, people skills can help you to make a positive difference. If you think of people who have made a lasting impression on you, you will probably discover that one thing they all have in common is good people skills. Don't allow the end of this book to be the end of your attention to this area of your development. It is only a part of the journey.

I believe that when I have finished developing my people skills, I will disappear in a flash of white light! In the meantime, I am enjoying the fascinating journey of continuing to explore how people tick, and I hope to meet you on the path.

SUGGESTED READING

Bach, Richard (1989) *The Tao of Pooh*, Mandarin, London.
 A delightful way to remind yourself of useful ways of being.
Covey, Stephen (1992) *The Seven Habits of Highly Effective People*, Simon & Schuster, London.
 A clear statement of how people can improve their own effectiveness.
Dyer, Wayne (1990) *You'll See It When You Believe It*, Arrow, London.
 Lovely and easy to read description of the powers of our beliefs.
Kamp, Di (1994) *The Dynamics of Excellence*, Di Kamp, Worcester.
 A set of audio-tapes that takes you through the techniques for developing your own potential and that of others.
Laborde, Genie (1987) *Influencing with Integrity*, Syntony Publishing, Palo Alto, California.
 An excellent book for developing your awareness of communication skills.
Peters, Tom (1989) *Thriving on Chaos*, Macmillan, London.
 A reminder of what we are likely to be facing in terms of workplace change and what we need to do to deal with it.

Peters, Tom (1994) *The Pursuit of Wow!*, Macmillan, London.
As he describes it, 'it's every person's guide to topsy-turvy times'.

Robbins, Anthony (1988) *Unlimited Power*, Simon & Schuster, London.
The simplest guide I know to empowerment of self and others.

Senge, Peter (1994) *The Fifth Discipline*, Doubleday, New York.
A practical guide to the new skills required in the future of work.

Tannen, Deborah (1989) *That's Not What I Meant*, Virago Press, London.
A useful description of how we misunderstand each other's communications.

Williams, Paul (1987) *Remember Your Essence*, Harmony Books, New York.
A gentle way of reminding yourself how to be at your best.

INDEX

Also from McGraw-Hill

79 / 80 Things You Must Do to be a Great Boss
David Freemantle

'One of my favourite handbooks.'
Kevin Keegan, Manager,
Newcastle United Football Club.
*For managers aiming to get the best out
of their people, this book is a must!*

ISBN: 0 07 709043 8
£12.95

Developing a Learning Culture
Sue Jones

*" highly practical book that should be read by all managers and
 iiners who are concerned with implementing change, strategies
 and collaborative teamworking."* Management Training.

ISBN: 0 07 707983 3
£19.95

---

01 Ways to Develop Your People Without Really Trying
Peter Honey

*Thousands of ideas on how to fit piggyback learning and
development on the shoulders of normal work activities.*

ISBN: 0 07 709183 3
£16.95

Dealing With People Problems at Work
Steven Palmer and Tim Burton

*A down-to-earth guide for managers in how to handle a range
of everyday people problems found in most work situations.
This book's practical step-by-step approach will help many who
find their work colleagues a palpable source of job stress."*
Gary Cooper, Manchester School of Management.

ISBN: 0 07 709177 9
£12.95

A Manager's Guide to Self-Development, Third Edition
Mike Pedler

*This working philosophy of
 self-development has become the
 pensable guide to helping managers
 ise their potential and improve their
 abilities and performance.*

ISBN: 0 07 707829 2
£14.95

Developing Managers as Coaches
Frank S. Salisbury

*Based on the view that everyone has a "seed of greatness",
this book will inspire you to leap forward into the crucial concept
of coaching in the business environment.*

ISBN: 0 07 707892 6
19.95

The Power of Personal Influence
Richard Hale

*"A most valuable book which provides a refreshingly practical
approach to improving all aspects of how we influence others."*
Wenche Marshall Foster, Chief Executive, Perrier Group.

ISBN: 0 07 709131 0
£14.95

Vision At Work
John Mitchell

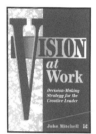

*Highlighting the link between strategy
and the decision-making process, this
book explores how creative leaders can
translate 'vision' into effective 'action'.*

ISBN: 0 07 709085 3
£19.95

Workplace Counselling
Di Kamp

*"Di Kamp is able to describe ways to bring out the best in people.
All that remains now is for the rest of us to implement the ideas."*
Rob Ball, Rover Group Ltd.

ISBN: 0 07 709152 3
£19.95

The Project Manager as Change Agent
J Rodney Turner

*"This text is required reading for all those involved and
interested in the management of change in the 90s."*
Eric Gabriel, Vice-President, Association of Project Managers.

ISBN: 0 07 707741 5
£24.95

The Handbook of Project-Based Management
J Rodney Turner

*A radical re-evaluation of the often overlooked role of the project
manager who has to maximise strategic and successful change.*

ISBN: 0 07 707656 7
£45.00

***Prices are correct at the time of going to press but are subject to change**

Available from all good bookshops

McGraw-Hill Publishing Company
Shoppenhangers Road, Maidenhead, Berkshire, SL6 2QL, England
Tel: ++44 (0) 1628 23431 / Fax: ++44 (0) 1628 35895